ENTERING THE SCHOOL OF THE PROPHETS

Training a Prophetic Generation

Scott Wallis

Lighthouse Publications

Entering the School of the Prophets
by Scott Wallis

Printed in the United States of America
ISBN 1-933656-04-2

Unless otherwise indicated, Bible quotations are taken from the King James Version.

Publisher
Lighthouse Publications
2028 Larkin Avenue
Elgin, IL 60123
(847) 697-6788
www.Lighthouse-Publications.com

Cover Design
Scott Wallis & Associates
2028 Larkin Avenue
Elgin, IL 60123
(847) 468-1457

Foreword

God called me into the prophetic ministry about twelve years ago. One day, while I was playing the piano and praising the Lord, and a strong wind entered the room. Believing this to be of the Lord I opened my Bible and my eyes fell to chapter 3 in the book of Ezekiel. As I read the words in this passage of scripture, I was sure that God was calling me into the ministry and personally talking to me. One verse that particularly stood out was Ezekiel 3:17 which says, "Son of man, I have made you a watchman unto the house of Israel: therefore hear the word at my mouth, and give them warning from me." At this moment in time, a feeling came into my heart that my life would never be the same.

After this life-changing experience, I told my mother what happened to me and how God called me into the ministry. I also told her, "Mother, I don't know when or where, but I know that I am not going to be in Brazil for too long." I was persuaded that God had something better for me than I had planned for myself. As such, I was filled with a sense of expectancy and faith looking for God to fulfill His Word to me. I began spending great amounts of time seeking the Lord. I wanted to find His will for my life. My search eventually led me to the baptism in the Holy Spirit.

One week after experiencing the baptism in the Holy Spirit, the devil tried to hurt or possibly kill me in a car accident. This happened on a Saturday evening. The next morning I went to a friend of mine who I consider to be a prophet and asked him to pray for me. I was really confused and scared about what had just happened. As this prophet of God began praying for me, God suddenly started using him in prophecy to speak to me. Part of the prophetic word that He shared with me was from the very passage in the book of Ezekiel that God had spoken to me a few months earlier.

This word of prophecy gave me a great deal of comfort and yet part of me was still filled with unbelief over what just happened. Less than ten minutes later, a friend of my friend's showed up at his house unexpectedly, he then asked his friend to pray for me. Without hesitation, his friend started praying for me with great boldness and in less than a minute he began prophesying to me. The Lord through this man began to rebuke me for my unbelief and said, "for you to know that this is the Lord talking to you, I am mentioning Ezekiel 3:17." That was powerful!

Within a couple of months a group of leaders came from London to hold a prophetic conference in Sao Paulo, Brazil. During the first meeting, approximately five hundred people were in the auditorium. One of the pastors opened the meeting in prayer. In His prayer, he began to prophecy regarding the meeting. Suddenly, he started to speak about Ezekiel 3:17. Almost nine months later (not realizing at the time), I understood this pastor was speaking to me; it was God confirming the call that He had placed upon my life.

The meetings held at this prophetic conference were awesome. God spoke numerous times and in a variety of ways to me throughout the course of the meetings. Some of the things God spoke to my heart during these prophetic meetings were about leaving Brazil, preaching and teaching the Word of God and the various stages that He would take me through to help me develop mental toughness as a soldier of Christ. This plus the tremendous signs and wonders that were taking place during the meeting confirmed so much to me about God's calling upon my life.

On the last day of the meeting, a funny feeling entered my heart about this group of leaders. I wanted to leave with them. I felt as if they were part of my family. Even though the meetings had grown to over eight hundred people, I felt an excitement about spending time with them. One of the things that I wanted to do on the final day of the meetings was spend time with Colin Dye, the pastor responsible for the prophetic team. At this time, my English was extremely poor; I only knew a few words in English. In spite of this, I made the decision to come down from the balcony while he was still praying for some people to give him a hug.

When I came close to him, he turned toward me. Immediately, I had a vision where I saw a white sheet covering me. Within seconds, I fell onto the floor under the power of God and he fell on top of me. After spending a few moments on the floor, both of us stood back to our feet. I hugged him and said to him, "Nice to meet you." He looked at me, his eyes seemed to penetrate my soul, and said, "See you in London." This along with several other words that I received convinced me that I was to leave Sao Paulo and go to London. Through the providence of God, in several months I was in London studying at the Kennsington Temple Bible School.

Attending this school was extremely important experience in my life. The training I received helped me learn how to understand and flow in the prophetic office. My time in this school ignited the flame of God in my spirit to be used by God as a prophet. As such, I believe the material contained in this book is essential for every person called to and/or involved in prophetic ministry. Moreover, those who would like to learn more about prophetic ministry will find a wealth of information contained in this book regarding prophets and prophetic ministry.

Pastor Scott Wallis, through his knowledge and experience, clarifies in this book many myths regarding the true nature of the life of a prophet. Moreover, he shows the importance of building healthy relationships between the pastoral and prophetic ministry, relationships which need to be established in trust and not in fear. With wisdom, he helps bring the office of prophet to another level, a level of excellence, and shows us with deep insight the need for training in the life of every prophet.

It is truly an eye opening experience to see where the prophetic ministry currently is today and where God originally intended it to be. I feel privileged to be one of the first ones to read this book, and I am greatly blessed to have Pastor Scott Wallis as both a friend and prophet in my life. May God richly bless this book and the School of the Prophets described herein.

Pastor Leyff Wenderson
Strong Tower Church
Sao Paulo, Brazil

Contents

• **Entering the School of the Prophets** •

Introduction

The year was 1987 and I had just received the calling to be a prophet. God had just visited me through an open vision (an open vision happens while your eyes are open), where I saw the glory of God. This supernatural experience caught me totally off guard. It happened suddenly and without warning, and I have no idea how long it remained in my room. I was surrounded by God's glory. To this day, I can still see it – the sight as brilliant as ten thousand suns all rolled up into one.

As you can imagine, this experience totally changed my life. I was stunned, astonished and excited all in one moment of time. I became a radical follower of Jesus. Everything that I did was for the purpose of growing closer to Him. I became consumed by the Word of God. The Bible was my constant companion. I read, studied and meditated upon His Word day and night. I was so hungry for more of God that nothing could satisfy me. I spent hours in prayer. I did everything I could to draw closer to Jesus.

This was my introduction into the realm of prophecy. Something was awakened in me that night. My eyes were opened to see beyond the veil of flesh into the realm of the Spirit. I was made so keenly sensitive to spiritual things that, for a time, I could not function. God had supercharged my spiritual senses, so I could function at a higher level than most people are aware exists. The hand of God had come upon me, so that I could fulfill my calling to be a prophet of the Most High.

I am a prophet of God. I have gone through the necessary training to stand in this office. God has sovereignly called and commissioned me to stand before His people and speak, "Thus says the Lord." I do not speak these words lightly, for I know both the good and evil of what they can do. God has raised me up, for such a time as this, to speak to His Church about the importance of the prophetic office to His kingdom purposes. This is the reason I am writing this book, to share with you how a prophet is made.

Becoming the Word We Speak

Prophets are made, not born. Why do I say this? Because, like every ministry gift, each prophet must go through the process of training to fulfill his or her calling. This is one of the reasons why so many people called as prophets are never commissioned into the office of prophet – they have not been willing to pay the price to be trained. As the Scripture says, *"For many are called but few are chosen"* (Matt. 22:14). This is especially true for those who are called as prophets.

Just because someone is called to be a prophet does not mean they are one. There is a big difference between *being* a prophet and wanting to be a prophet. Wanting to be a prophet does not make us one, neither does speaking a prophetic word. One can prophesy all day under the anointing of the spirit of prophecy, and yet still not be a prophet. He or she may be a good prophesier, and yet, still not be a prophet. This holy office is reserved for holy men and women who become the word they speak.

Becoming the word we speak means that we have united our hearts with God's heart to such a degree that there is no difference between what *we* say and what *He* is saying (Rev. 19:10). The heart of the prophetic office is about becoming the prophetic word being spoken, so that it is possible to be proper spokesmen for the word. The place where we must go in our quest to enter and fulfill the prophetic office is the hidden place of the heart.

Being a prophet is more than just speaking a word from God. It is about communicating the heart of God. As a prophet, I am called to represent the heart of God to His people. What I share with people from the heart of God is as important, or more so, than what I speak to them prophetically. So then, being a prophet means that I have the ability to accurately represent the heart of God to those around me both in word and deed. If I do this, then I am truly a prophet of Almighty God.

To be able to do this, those called to be prophets are required to go through an intense training period. Some have called this training process "the PITs" (prophets in training). Being one who has gone through the PITs, I would have to agree with them that it can be the pits, literally. Going through God's prophetic training school is not fun; it can be extremely difficult and is often filled with unusual circumstances as well as events so bizarre that in many ways they are stranger than fiction.

This is what happened to me. One day, I received an open vision detailing my calling and destiny as a prophet. The next, I was bombarded with satanic opposition to this newfound call of God upon my life. I was nowhere near prepared for what happened to me. I felt like Dorothy in the Wizard of Oz: I was not in Kansas anymore. The weirdest things started happening to me – things that, to this day, I still wonder if they really happened to me.

This was my initiation into God's standard for training prophets. I felt dazed, hazed and amazed all in a moment. God took me by the hand and led me through what I am about to share with you in this book – the "School of the Prophets."

The School of the Prophets

What is a School of the Prophets? It is a place where prophets are trained to speak the word of God fearlessly and compassionately from the heart of God. They are taught to hear, speak and obey the voice of God without hesitation. It is a place of faith, hope and love – a place where we are launched to spread our wings upon the winds of the Spirit. God takes us beneath the shadow of His wing to train us to walk in His ways and carry forth His word to the ends of the earth.

The school of prophets was started in the days of Samuel and has its roots in the faith of our father, Abraham. Abraham is the first man in Scripture who is called a prophet. This speaks volumes about what the prophetic office entails.

The life of Abraham was a life of faith, vision and destiny, and this is what all prophets are called to carry on earth. And yet, there is more, for Abraham was not only a prophet of God, he was the friend of God. This is the destination for all those called into the office of prophet.

As such, the office of prophet is about intimacy and friendship with God. It is this intimacy that enables a man or woman to speak unashamedly for God. God anoints those who walk with Him in the secret place of prayer. It is as we walk in this secret place of prayer, that we are schooled to speak prophetically for God. God trains us to hear, know and follow His voice in the secret place of prayer. As such, all prophets must be pray-ers.

The school of prayer precedes the School of the Prophets and is the birthplace for every genuine prophet and all genuine prophetic ministry. We cannot enroll in the School of the Prophets, unless we have first entered the school of prayer. Prayer is to the ministry of prophets what water is to a fish – their source of life. Prayer is the source of the prophet's life and power with God and man. Without prayer, a prophet is without the life that only the Spirit of God can bring.

The School of the Prophets is a place where we learn how to live and move in the Holy Spirit. The person of the Holy Spirit becomes our guide, helper and companion in life and ministry. We learn how to flow with Him and follow Him along the path of life. He becomes our teacher, our lives are the classroom and the Bible is the text. We are taught His ways and learn to think His thoughts. As we tune into Him – what He is saying and what He is doing, His presence fills our lives.

This is what fills prophecy with life – God's life. The life of God flows from the union of the prophet with the Holy Spirit. When we are in tune with the Holy Spirit, His life flows through us and the words we speak. This is why we must learn how to keep an ear tuned to what the Holy Spirit is saying. Anything less can be devastating to the prophet, his ministry and those to whom he ministers. Truly, a prophet must learn to live "... by every word that proceeds from the mouth of God."

This is why those called to be prophets need the training that comes in a School of the Prophets. We need to learn how to live by the proceeding word of God. This means more than just hearing His voice; it means learning what He has said and how to apply what He has said in simple obedience. It is this implicit obedience to the proceeding word of God that enables those who are called to be prophets to become those who are commissioned to the office of prophet.

Speaking the Words of God

This commission is a significant event in the life of a prophet. When Christ commissions a prophet, there comes an unusual grace upon his or her life. This grace releases to them the ability to speak on behalf of the Lord. It gives them unprecedented favor in the eyes of God and man. It is this favor that paves the way for them to speak the word of the Lord. Without this favor from God, they will be speaking as it were to deaf ears, because no one will listen to them.

God is the one who gives people an ear to hear what a prophet is saying. Even if this prophet is speaking what the people do not want to hear, they will listen, because mankind cannot avoid the voice of God. They will either accept or reject it. The Holy Spirit is the one who empowers the words that a prophet speaks, and it is in the School of the Prophets where an impartation of power is made for a prophet to speak the word of God with power.

Speaking the word of God with power is essential for all those who are called to minister as prophets. This is why every prophet must be trained and/or connected to a School of the Prophets. God will use this school to empower His prophets through a divine charge of grace. This charge of grace energizes the prophetic words spoken and enables prophets to look adversity in the face without fear. Only God can do this in the life of His prophets, as we spend time with senior prophets.

Senior prophets are those who have been called and commissioned by God to raise up Schools of Prophets. Senior prophets are men or women who are fathers or mothers in the faith, and are graced to teach those who hear them to walk in the ways of God's grace. This is why the Schools of the Prophets are called "the sons of the prophets" in the Scriptures. These schools are founded and fathered by senior prophets who teach their spiritual sons to walk in the ways of God.

Because, of this, prophets will often take on the characteristic of the spiritual fathers who fathered them. This was true in the case of Elisha. Elisha knew his spiritual father was Elijah. Elijah had many sons, but only one of them was ready to follow in his footsteps – Elisha. Because, Elisha was ready to follow in his spiritual fathers footsteps, God gave him a double portion of the anointing upon Elijah. The Scriptures tell us that the same spirit that was upon Elijah came upon Elisha.

This is the promise of God for those who enter a School of the Prophets: they will be propelled farther as prophets, faster than they could have gone themselves. God will open doors that no man can shut and He will shut doors that no man can open. Opportunities that would have passed us by will open before us, for God will anoint us to walk through these open doors of opportunity. Adversities we would have faced will fall before us because of the anointing of God that rests upon us through our connection with a School of the Prophets.

Get ready! We are living in a new day, and God is raising up Schools of the Prophets all across the earth. I, myself, am one who is called to be a part of this by teaching others the things that the Lord has taught me regarding the prophetic office and ministry. I hope that you will open your ears to hear what the Holy Spirit is saying through me in this book. The time has come for God's prophets to arise – this is our shining hour and

the release of God's prophetic power. Are you
ready?

Chapter One

The Prophet's Call

T he prophet's call is one of the most misunderstood things in the Body of Christ today. Many believe that, for a person to be a prophet, they have to have a dramatic call like the one I described in the last chapter. And yet, this is completely untrue. In the same way a man or woman is called into ministry as a pastor teacher or evangelist, so also they can be called as a prophet.

The calling to be a prophet can come in many different ways. For some, it may be an open vision, as I described in the last chapter. For others, it may be an inward witness, where they just know this is what God has called them to do. There are probably as many ways that God can call someone into the office of prophet, as there are people. Each prophet's calling is special and significant to their ministry, and can often reveal several distinct factors about their calling.

One of the reasons God calls prophets the way He does is so that each prophet can individually learn how to fulfill their unique calling. There are several different ways in which people learn. Some people are visual learners – they learn by seeing. Others are auditory learners – they learn by listening. Still, others are kinetic learners – they learn by doing. God takes all these things into consideration when He calls someone into the prophet's office. This is why there are so many different Hebrew words describing the office of prophet in Scripture.

Not all prophets are the same. We, as individuals, can be called into the same office, and yet, be completely different in the way we function in this ministry. As such, it is important for prophets to learn early that they are many different kinds of prophets, and none of them is more special to God than the others. This can be a difficult thing to teach, especially in our day where the more dramatic the call, the greater the entertainment factor to people.

Generally, people are fascinated by the supernatural, and what could be more

4

supernatural than hearing from God the way some prophets do. I have heard of prophets having open visions, trances, audible voices, angelic visitations, visitations from Jesus, translations, and the list goes on. We are filled with a sense of wonder and awe when God does something like this, and we are drawn to it. There is nothing wrong with this. But, it is wrong to think this is the way all prophets should be or that these visitations make some prophets greater than others.

A Higher Standard

One of the things that I have noticed, as a prophet among prophets, is that prophets tend to congregate around their gifting. This creates a sense of exclusion for others who are still called to be prophets, but not in the same way as those already in "the club." This mentality is as worldly as it gets, and yet, many prophets have come to base the way they view prophets through this kind of thinking. As such, much of what God is saying gets lost in the drama of the prophetic, and the purpose for the prophet is tainted.

This is extremely important for us to understand as prophets. We need to know how people are going to react to us, because we are prophesying to people. Not everyone will esteem us highly. Some people will question our motives and our words. Some will call us on those things we are doing or saying. Some will easily buy into the things we are saying or doing, even if we are wrong. Some will depend on us so much that they will lose sight of Jesus, the One Who died for them. These things can be deadly, if, and when, they happen.

Remember, although we minister to people, we are responsible to God. God is holding His prophets to a higher standard of integrity and accountability, and sometimes He will use people to do this. This can be very difficult for many prophets to hear, especially those who believe they have a good track record in hearing God. Why is this? Because, we become so accustomed to the voice of God we hear, that we miss the voice of God that we don't hear.

Building Positive Relationships

Prophets don't often consider the fact that they selectively hear what God is saying to them – this is why we prophesy in part. No prophet has the complete story from God, even if we think we see everything clearly. God gives His prophets different pieces of the same puzzle so that we can learn to work with one another in putting these pieces together. This is why being able to build quality long-lasting relationships is vital to our ability as prophets to fulfill our prophetic calling.

Most prophets do not realize how important their relationships are to their prophetic call. This is one of the main reasons many prophets fall short in fulfilling the calling on their lives. There are many prophets who have been genuinely called by God but never commissioned by Him, because they never learned how to relate properly to people. When this happens, a person called to be a prophet can be swept into doctrinal and other delusions. These delusions, if left unchecked, build an impenetrable wall of isolation.

Total isolation is a deadly enemy to a prophet. The enemy loves to isolate prophets from people through misunderstandings. This is how he will usually attack those called to be prophets. The enemy uses these misunderstandings to create confusion regarding the validity of the person called as a prophet. This confusion, if left unchecked, can damage the credibility of the person called as a prophet. When this happens, people will not regard what the prophet says, even if he or she is right.

I have personally experienced this in my calling as a prophet. I have been greatly misunderstood even by those who are close to me. There have been times when I have said things to people, and they heard something totally different than what I said. Because, of this, I have learned there are times when we need to confront the perceptions that people have, especially when they are untrue. We cannot let sleeping dogs lie; otherwise we will end up getting bitten by them or trip over them.

This is why being in right relationship with others becomes so important to the prophet. When a prophet has good relationships with others, he will usually have a more stable outlook on life. This creates a place of accountability and integrity for the prophet, a place where he is not surrounded by people who will continually say "yes" to him. This kind of honesty in relationships is an extremely good place for prophet, because it protects them from the enemy's plan to isolate them from others.

I am extremely grateful to God for the people that He has placed in my life; they have made me a better person and prophet. I have learned how to love and live with people, and yet be the man that God has called me to be. These things are not isolated, they are interconnected. We are as good at being prophets as our relationship skill allow us to be in relating to people. We can only turn people to God to the degree that we love them as they are in our lives. This is a crucial building block in being a genuine prophet.

I believe that one of the main reasons why we have had such problems in prophetic ministries over the past few years is because of the lack of relationship among many of today's prophets. We have seen this as part of the prophet's ministry, rather than an unhealthy personality trait. As a result, prophets have become reclusive, seclusive and exclusive in their thinking. Prophets who succumb to this kind of thinking have fallen from the lofty place of being God's spokesman to the lowly place of hermithood.

Prophetic Beginnings

The prophet is a spokesman for the Almighty; he is in an exalted position before both God and man. As such, he should command great respect from those around them. The quality of his character is what paves the way for the words he speaks to be heard. This is why prophets need to learn how to live their lives before both God and man. They must know how and when to speak, so as to bless and not curse those who hear them. To do this, a prophet must go through extensive training in God's school for prophets.

What is a School of the Prophets? A School of the Prophets is a place where prophets who are called learn how to fulfill their calling in the context of working with others who are also called. As they progress and become seasoned in God's School of the Prophets, they are released into their commission. This commission is an assignment entrusted to the prophet by God that he is to fulfill in the corporate setting of the Church. When this happens, great blessing will follow the prophet and his ministry.

The Schools of the Prophets began prior to Samuel's birth and probably started during the days of Moses. This means that the Schools of the Prophets were functioning well before Samuel time in Israel. And yet, Samuel's life is of strategic significance in that he raised up several Schools of Prophets during his lifetime. This, plus the fact that he anointed the first and second kings in Israel, reveals the importance of Samuel's life to Israel's history. Samuel left a legacy through his prophetic ministry that went on for generations.

When we come to the days of Elijah and Elisha, we see these same Schools of Prophets built up during the days of Samuel still operating. And, we see Elijah functioning in the role of a spiritual father or senior prophet. Elijah amazingly comes from nowhere to lead the Schools of the Prophets through one of its most difficult periods. In a dramatic display of God's power, Elijah prophesies to Ahab, *"There shall be neither dew nor rain these years according to my word"* (1 Kings 17:1).

This is the beginning of Elijah's ministry. Prior to this time, nothing is said about Elijah. What we do know is that, later in Elijah's life, he becomes the leader of the Schools of the Prophets. This gives us a good indication of where Elijah was prior to this power encounter with Ahab. He was probably being trained as a prophet among the Schools of the Prophets. Elijah had been the son of a prophet before he became a prophet, and then a father, among prophets.

A Prophet's Need for Training

What I have just said cuts clear against the grain of modern thinking regarding the prophet's ministry. Our present view of prophets falls far short of the picture painted in Scripture. We view

11

prophets as individuals who are one day called by God to speak, and the next day raised up into a position to speak. This popular notion leaves little need or room for prophets to be trained or schooled in ministry. This is not only unscriptural – it is downright foolish.

Prophets need to be trained before they are commissioned into ministry. God will commission those who are trained, not train those who are commissioned. The commission comes after the training. This is why we need to attend God's school for prophets, so that we can fulfill the call of Christ upon our lives. When we do this, nothing will be able to stop us from fulfilling our destiny in Christ, except our own inability to walk in the character of Christ.

The School of the Prophets is a place where our character is formed and our lives are conformed into the image of Christ the prophet. I believe it is essential for each person called to the prophetic office to enter God's school of prophets for their own good. A School of the Prophets will keep us out of many troubles and enable us to leave a legacy that is pleasing to God. This way, our lives will not run aground, and we will not be shipwrecked upon the shores of life.

My desire in writing this book is to keep you from a myriad of troubles that presently afflict the prophetic office. I am doing this to raise the standard of excellence among God's prophets. I want to release among prophets the knowledge, wisdom and understanding that God has given to me regarding how a School of the Prophets is called to function and the purposes behind it. This understanding will, I believe, help many fulfill their calling to be prophets in the Church for years to come – at least this is my hope.

Chapter Two

• **Entering the School of the Prophets** •

16

The Prophet's Office

I believe that one of the most misunderstood subjects in the Body of Christ today is the office of prophet. Some have questioned whether prophets really exist today. Others have questioned the degree of authority given to the prophet. Still others have made the prophet a demigod, and will do nothing without the approval of the prophet. In reality, none of these ideas about the prophet are Scripturally based, but instead are based upon conjecture, myth and superstition.

Being a prophet myself, this kind of misinformation concerns me. Wrong perceptions regarding prophets produce unhealthy models for budding prophets to follow. When budding prophets follow an unhealthy ministry model, they will inevitably bring reproach upon the ministry of the prophet and the gospel of Christ. This further brings reproach upon those prophets who are truly hearing from God and doing His will within the Church.

As such, I believe it is important for me to bring clarity of understanding to the training processes through which the Lord leads His prophets prior to their commission. Every called prophet will be trained in some way for the ministry to which they are called prior to their commission. Some will go through the "school of hard knocks," and learn what they need to know through the trials of life. Others will attend Bible College, and then find their way through the "school of hard knocks." Still others will enter a school for prophets, and through their training, avoid many of the pitfalls that prophets often experience in the "school of hard knocks."

Regardless of where the prophet is trained, every true prophet will be trained prior to their commission. What I want you to understand is this: The place where a prophet receives their training only determines the level of pain endured through the training process not the quality of the training received.

18

I believe it is essential for us to understand the training processes through which God take His prophets. I will talk about this in greater detail later in this book. However, before I talk about these training processes, I want to provide some general information regarding the prophet's office. In this chapter, I will share with you some vital teachings about various areas of the prophet's office, such as the authority of the prophet, the different kinds of prophets and their mode of revelation, what the prophet is called to do in the Church, and how their ministry is to function with the other ministry gifts in the Church. I will do this to provide a clearer picture of how a genuine prophet should function in the Church today.

God Uses Imperfect Vessels

We have already seen that prophets can be called into ministry through a variety of ways. Some prophets will be called through open visions, angelic visitations or visitations by the Lord. These things are not uncommon for those called to be prophets. Yet, some prophets may be called through more mundane methods, such as an inward witness, prophetic illumination through Scripture, personal prophecy from another prophet, or providential guidance through circumstances.

One of the dangers within the prophet's office is for those called into ministry through these more dramatic visitations to become puffed up with pride over the way in which God called them. If this happens, a prophet can begin putting down other prophets, ministers or believers who have not received such a dramatic visitation. In the end, prophets who become filled with this kind of pride can begin thinking their words are more authoritative than those other prophets receive. In some cases, pride can so fill their hearts that they begin thinking God has given them a special place of privileged authority because they receive open visions, audible words or angelic visitations. The reality is that the type of revelation received does not determine the authority of the word or the person speaking.

The greatest prophetic word ever spoken is contained in what has been canonized in the Holy Scriptures for all mankind. The Bible applies to the whole of humanity and cannot pass away without being completely fulfilled before Jesus comes again. This is the awesome reality of the Bible – it is a forever settled Word that contains final authority for all practices in the Church.

20

When rightly understood, it is full and complete and without peer for understanding the way to heaven and the ways of heaven. Every prophetic word is subject to this Word, and none may violate its holy contents without being found false.

The greatest prophet who ever lived revealed fully the nature, character, emotions and words of His Father without fault. This person was the Lord Jesus Christ. Every prophet in the Church today is called to pattern his or her life after the Lord Jesus Christ, for He is the ultimate Word. The Bible, speaking about Him says, *"God... hath in these last days spoken unto us by His Son..."* (Heb. 1:1-2).

Jesus, the Living Word, was and is the greatest Prophetic Word ever spoken (Rev. 19:10). The Bible says of Him: *"And the Word was made flesh and dwelt among us..."* (Jn. 1:14). Jesus, the Living Word of God, came to earth to live among men to communicate the words of His Father to all of mankind. Jesus fully communicated every word that His Father spoke without fault. In other words, He never "missed it" – none of His words ever fell to the ground. Moreover, He fully expressed the Father in every action, word, thought and deed.

No other prophet can fully express the mind will and heart of God like Jesus did. Speaking of prophets and prophecy, the Bible says, *"For we know in part, and we prophesy in part"* (1 Cor. 13:9). Every prophet prophesies in part, revealing details as he or she is graced by the will of the Father. As such, prophets today are fallible and can make mistakes in the prophecies given in word, interpretation or action. For true prophets, this is never our intention. Rather, it happens because we are imperfect vessels.

So then, any prophet claiming equal authority with Scripture or the Son would be a false prophet. No true prophet today would claim this kind of authority in dealing with people. Yet, prophets do have authority to speak to the Church and the world. God has never stopped the mouths of His prophets; He merely changed the requirements for the giving and receiving of prophetic words. God will and does hold His prophets accountable, as well as the people who listen to them.

A Functional Role in the Church

Speaking of prophetic accountability, the Bible says, *"Let the prophets speak two or three and let the other(s) judge"* (1 Cor. 14:29). Some have interpreted this verse to mean that any other people present in the service, including the pastor, are to judge the prophetic word. Although I think this may be a good practice to follow, it isn't what Paul is teaching. In this passage of Scripture, he is specifically teaching the believers in Corinth how prophets should function in the Church.

Hence, from Scripture, we are taught that prophets should be given a functional role in the Church. Accordingly, they have authority from God to minister within the Church prophetically. God has set prophets in the Church, and in so doing He has given them authority to edify and equip the Church to hear the voice of God. The Church cannot function properly without the ministry of the prophet. And, anyone seeking to circumvent or frustrate the ministry of prophets in the Church today is not only doing a disservice to the Church, but also hindering the very work of God in our day.

Knowing these facts about prophets provides us with a foundational understanding of the prophetic office. So then, prophets have authority to function in the Church in the realm of prophecy. Some have limited the prophetic office to this realm, believing in the functionality of the ministry of prophecy, but not in its ability to govern the Church. And yet, my question to those who believe this is: Would God really limit His prophets to only function in this fashion – speaking prophetically at the whim of a pastor or leader?

Somehow, I think not. Prophets are more than prophesiers. In this context, prophesiers are those who receive revelation from God, but are not called into the office of prophet. Prophesiers may receive revelation from God, but will rarely provide the necessary wisdom to discern what this revelation means to the Church. Prophesiers may receive visions, revelations, visitations and yet still not be prophets. Prophets who have been commissioned by Christ to function in an office are foundational and functional governmental headship ministries to the Church. This is the main difference between a prophesier (the gift) and a prophet (the office).

Moreover prophets are more than parachurch ministries who do not have authority in the Church. Christ has set prophets in the Church and given them governmental authority to function in this office. I believe Jesus desires for His prophets to have the room they need to do what He has called them to do. When prophets

24

are functioning as a normal part of the Church, as they should, the life and health of the Church is greatly enriched, and many problems being faced by the Church are immediately remedied and rectified.

So then, prophets have governmental authority in the Church. Christ has set prophets in the Church to work with the leadership of the Church in building the Church. For prophets to function in the Church effectively, time and room must be made for them to do what they are called to do. In other words, prophets and prophetic ministry should not relegated to function in the back room of the Church all the time. There should be a time and place set aside for prophets to function in the Church. As long as prophets remain sidelined by pastors and leaders, the Church will be sidelined from effectively doing the work of Christ.

If prophets have governmental authority within the Church and this is the primary means by which we understand whether a man or woman is truly called to be a prophet, why then are so few prophets functioning in the Church this way? Simple: the Church has lacked understanding in this area, not being taught what the Word of God actually teaches about the prophetic office. Many pastors and leaders have taught that prophets are only traveling ministers, who rarely help with the foundational elements of the local church. In reality, nothing could be further from the truth.

Being Connected To Christ's Church

Remember, prophets are foundational to the Church. This means Christ has given them supernatural understanding in how the local Church should function. A local church may exist without prophets but it will never function, as it should, without the ministry of a prophet. Does this mean that every local church should have a prophet? No, but it does mean that every local church should be rightly related to prophets that are speaking authoritatively into those things being done by the local church to fulfill its call.

Pastors are to be rightly related to prophets so that prophets may use their prophetic insight to help in building the local church. A local church needs prophets who are rightly related with pastors to bring guidance, direction and accountability to pastors and their flocks. This is how the office of prophet is to function in the local church. Prophets and pastors are to be submitted, one to another, for the purpose of establishing the Word and will of God within the local church.

When this happens, the local church grows and is edified, and believers begin entering and fulfilling their destiny in Christ. A healthier, happier church blesses the pastor and his flock, and the prophet, after he leaves, should be blessed and supported by this same pastor and church. This is the way God designed the pastor and prophet to work together for the mutual edification of one another and in building the local church.

God wants members of His Church to function as He designed them. When pastors and prophets work together, this becomes possible. As a result, pastors and prophets are a vital ministry combination that can help one another to fulfill God's will and vision for their lives. The pastor helps the prophet by providing resources, and the prophet helps the pastor by providing revelation. Each minister brings what they have to the edification of the other.

Why then do prophets and pastors often struggle with one another? This can happen because the pastor doesn't appreciate what the prophet brings, or the prophet doesn't appreciate what the pastor brings. If prophets don't appreciate what the pastor brings, they will lose a vital connection that could help them expand the kingdom of Christ. If pastors don't appreciate what the prophet brings, they lose the revelation knowledge they need to effectively build the church, and as a result, the church suffers.

Could it be that many churches among us are sick and dying because of this fact? Maybe, by not discerning the importance of prophets, pastors have left themselves open to the attacks of the enemy. Pastors today are leaving the ministry at an alarming rate. Most pastors will never enter into a time fruitful ministry, according to George Barna, a leading expert in analyzing church statistics. Could this be one of the reasons why so many pastors are leaving the ministry disillusioned and discouraged? They have not received the ministry of prophets.

Turning People from Sin

Being a prophet can be a tough proposition today. Many believers do not want to hear a true Word from the Lord. Does this alarm you? I say this with years of experience ministering to pastors, leaders and believers who only want to hear positive affirmations from God and are unwilling to listen to any form of correction or reproof for sin. This is a real problem in the Church because prophets are called to bring more than superficial words of blessing; they are called to bring real blessing by turning people away from sin. Sin is the primary destroyer of God's blessing upon our lives. This is why every prophet should hate sin.

Prophets are to turn people away from sin. This is one of God's primary purposes for prophets and prophetic ministry. A prophet who does not turn people away from sin is not really functioning as a prophet. Sometimes prophets are called to turn people away from sin by exposing it. On the other hand, most of the time, prophets turn people away from sin by pointing them in the right direction. Providing clear prophetic guidance to someone heading in the wrong direction will often enable them to do what is right. This is wisdom.

Wisdom is an essential ingredient to those functioning in the office of prophet. A prophet without wisdom will eventually cause great harm to people and, in the end, damage the work of God. This is why learning how to receive wisdom is so important to the prophet. A prophet must be able to inquire of the Lord and receive specific instructions for individual situations. This is part of what makes a prophet an effective prophet. Oftentimes, people will come to prophets lacking wisdom or direction for their lives. A prophet needs to be able to supply them with the godly wisdom they need to do God's will for their lives.

Ears to Hear

Inquiring of the Lord is a very important part to being an effective prophet. David, one of the best known and most beloved leaders and prophets in Israel, would do nothing unless he inquired of the Lord. David learned how to tune in to what God was saying by inquiring of Him. Once he heard what God was saying for a specific situation, he would then diligently follow what God said for the purpose of bringing glory to God. Every prophet needs to be able, at all times, to hear what God is saying. The way prophets do this is by cultivating an attitude in their heart that says, *"Speak Lord, for your servant hears"* (1 Sam. 3:9). Prophets should always have an ear listening to hear what God is saying.

Just because all prophets hear from God, this does not mean they all hear the same thing in the same way. Much of the confusion regarding the prophet and his ministry exists because of this misunderstand. It can be easy to expect every prophet to receive the same revelation from God in the same way. When this doesn't happen, it can cause people to question what the validity of what a prophet has said. Knowing that prophets will often receive different revelations in different ways enables people to look beyond the way a prophet ministered to the actual content of the words that were ministered.

Moreover, the way in which a revelation is received or ministered does not determine its authority. I believe this is a major fallacy being taught by those within the prophetic movement today. Many who are seers will often teach that their visions have greater authority or validity than the revelations received or ministered by an auditory prophet. As such, seers can think that visual revelation is the highest form of revelation. This is not true, and is one of the main reasons why some seer prophets have had such a difficult time relating to other types of prophets.

I have noticed in my dealings with different prophetic ministries within the Body of Christ that visual prophets will often say to auditory prophets, "You shouldn't say, 'Thus saith the Lord.'" When this happens, auditory prophets will begin to defend how they minister, for they know it is from the Lord. Auditory prophets are called to prophesy by grace through faith. Seer prophets are called to speak forth what they see by faith. The way a revelation is received does not make it more or less valid or spiritual.

God set different ministries in the Body so that we could complement one another. Auditory and visual prophets are to complement one another. For this to happen, prophets need to learn how to work with one another. As such, auditory prophets need to learn how to hear what visual prophets are seeing, and visual prophets need to learn how to see what auditory prophets are speaking. By prophets beginning to learn how to work with other prophets, it will move everyone called into the prophetic office toward a greater level of maturity.

Five Different Kinds of Prophets

How can prophets begin to learn how to work with one another? By understanding the various modes of revelations available to those called as prophets. The different modes of revelations given to prophets enable them to understand the full spectrum of what God is saying. God may speak to one prophet, give a vision to another prophet, share His burden with another prophet and

32

illuminate certain thoughts to another prophet. Each of these prophets may have received a genuine revelation from God, and as such, have a piece of what God is seeking to communicate. Therefore, we need to learn how to hear what God is saying through the various ways in which He seeks to communicate with us so that we might gain a more perfect understanding of what He is speaking to us. This is what some have called, "seeking the whole counsel of God."

The Scriptures reveal five different main categories of prophets. These prophets are identified through the mode of revelation received. There are five different Hebrew words used in reference to prophets or prophecy:

- Roeh
- Chozeh
- Nabi
- Nataf
- Massa

Each Hebrew word emphasizes a different way in which prophets receive revelation from God. As such, knowing what each word means is vital to our understanding of the prophet's office.

Roeh: The Seer

The first word we will examine is the word Roeh that literally means Seer. This kind of prophet sees the revelations he receives from God visually. Seers see what God is saying or doing in the spiritual realm and then prophesy or proclaim what they see being done through prophetic words or acts. Often, Roeh prophets will see angels, demons or even Christ Himself. Seers will often see things before they happen through prophetic foresight. When this happens, they will visually see things happening or themselves doing something through spiritual eyes.

When what they see begins to happen in the natural, Seers will need to act out what they saw happen in the spirit. By acting out what they saw, miracles will often take place in response to their acts of faith. Seers are called to speak prophetically what they see by faith and then do what they saw themselves do by faith. This is the way Seers are called to receive and walk in the revelation given them by God.

Chozeh: The Thinker

The next Hebrew word, Chozeh, means to gaze. This describes a prophet who can see what God is saying through the eyes of his/her heart.

34

Prophets called to function this way can receive revelations through a trance and/or an internal vision or knowing. Most of the time, what Chozeh prophets receive are internal knowings about what God is saying. These knowings are actually the Chozeh prophet thinking the very thoughts of God. God literally infuses this type of prophet with His own thoughts regarding specific topics and/or areas of concern. In this process, God communicates these specific thoughts to the mind of the prophet through a single or series of revelations or illuminations of God's purposes.

Nabi: The Speaker

The third Hebrew word for prophet is Nabi and means to bubble up. This describes a prophet who speaks forth what they hear little by little. A Nabi prophet will rarely hear or see things before they begin prophesying. As such, they will almost always prophesy by grace through faith. God gives the Nabi prophet a word to start with, and as he/she faithfully speaks what God has already given to him/her God will give him/her more. This prophetic flow will usually continue until the Nabi prophet has finished speaking what they believe God is saying.

Nataf: The Amplifier

The next Hebrew word for prophet is Nataf, which means to fall as the rain. In other words, the Nataf prophet's words literally open the windows of heaven for us to hear from God. The Nataf prophet's words fall like the rain upon our lives touching us with a refreshing sense of God's presence. This means their prophecies are not localized through what they are speaking; instead others will often hear what God is saying to them for themselves as the Nataf prophet speaks. God literally uses a Nataf prophets words as a conduit for His presence and voice to be heard by others. As a Nataf prophet speaks, revelation and illumination enters the heart and mind of the individual, so that they begin understanding what God is saying to them about specific situations or areas in their lives.

Massa: The Burden Bearer

The last Hebrew word for prophet is Massa, and means a burden from the Lord. This speaks to the weight of the revelation that God gives to a Massa prophet. Often, their words will contain an overwhelming call to prayer or repentance. The Massa prophet is a burden-bearer, who prays over every word received. Their prophetic words will almost always contain a burden or call to pray about specific situations. Usually others will feel the weight of what they are sharing while they are speaking, so as to come alongside and help them intercede over the burden received.

Each prophet and prophetic word shared is important to the heart of God. A prophet's words contain great significance to those who hear what they say. When any prophet speaks, their words are the words of God, and as such, should be heard and heeded. What happens in our lives could very well be determined by whether or not we listen to what one of these prophets says. No matter how or through whom God chooses to speak to us, we need to be open to what He is saying.

Prophets are important to the heart of God. God longs to communicate with us, individually and corporately. As such, he has provided various types of prophets so that we might gain His counsel regarding His specific will for our lives. If we are open to hearing what God is saying through His prophets, our lives become easier, clearer and less complicated. If, on the other hand, we are always drawn to the spectacular ways in which God speaks, we will almost certainly miss His supernatural workings in our lives.

Receiving God's Grace and Blessing

God wants to bless us. Prophets are one vehicle through which He can bless us. God has designed His prophets to bring His people into new realms of His grace. When prophets speak prophetically, they are releasing the grace of God into our lives. I don't know about you, but I need all the grace that God is willing to give to me. If we want to receive the grace that prophets can bring, we need to learn how to humble ourselves so that we can receive from them the words they are called to speak.

The prophet's office is a vital avenue whereby God's grace can enter the Church. Without this office, the Church suffers greatly, and many within the Church miss out on God's greater blessings for their lives. God doesn't want this to happen to His people, and neither do I. My encouragement to those in pastoral positions within the church is this: Receive prophets and prophecy into the church. Allow called prophets the time they need to be trained in Schools of Prophets, so they may be commissioned into their office and role as a prophet.

Prophets need to be released into their rightful place in the Church so that the Church may be edified by their words. This will not happen overnight, but will happen as called prophets are released into their prophetic office by senior prophets. Senior Prophets and their Schools of Prophets enable called prophets to grow in their ability to serve the Church in the prophetic office. I speak as a pastor to pastors, if we want the blessing prophets bring to the church, we must give them the room they need to grow in their ability to walk in and fulfill this office.

Grace is the essential ingredient in this process. Pastors must learn to give prophets grace so prophets can grow in their calling and then in turn bring God's grace to the church. This is the way God intended prophecy to function in the church. God wants prophets to begin serving Him in the capacity to which He has called them in the church. Prophets and prophecy are important to the heart of God. Those who help in this process of restoring prophets and prophecy to their rightful place within the Church can expect to receive God's richest blessings upon their lives. This is the promise of God to all choose to support His work of restoring prophets to His Church by raising up Schools of Prophets around the world. Lord, raise up a company of prophets, through powerful Schools of Prophets! Amen!

• The Prophet's Office •

Chapter Three

The Prophet's School

I love being a prophet. I am grateful to God that He called me into this ministry. I enjoy what I do, speaking the word of God into the lives of others. There is nothing quite as fun to me as being a prophet. I can't imagine what else I would do if there were no such thing as prophets. It would be like being a fish without water. And yet, my enthusiasm about being a prophet hasn't always been like this, especially when I was going through the "PITs."

Every prophet, no matter who they are, will go through the PITs. The PITs, as we have talked about previously, means that we are "Prophets In Training." Being a prophet in training is totally different from being a prophet who has been commissioned by Christ. And yet, in order to come to the place of being commissioned, every prophet who is called must go through the painful process of training. The Scriptures call this place of training the "School of the Prophets."

The School of the Prophets was a place of sonship. This is why the Schools of the Prophets were often called the sons of the prophets. Elder prophets would take younger prophets under their wing for the purpose of training them to function as prophets. Being the son of a well-known prophet was both a place of great honor and humiliation. Those who went through this process of becoming a prophet's son were often subjected to grueling work designed to break them of their pride.

Pride is a called prophet's greatest enemy. The enemy seeks to lead us to believe that we, by ourselves, can fulfill our calling. This is why so many who are genuinely called have failed in their calling; they were unwilling to come into a place of dependence upon God. And yet, this place of dependence upon God is essential for a prophet to learn, for it is in this place of dependence that we learn how to humble ourselves under the mighty hand of God, so that He may exalt us in due season.

Our season of exaltation is greatly dependent upon our season of humiliation. Unless we go through this process of humbling ourselves under the hand of God, we cannot be exalted to speak the Word of God to the nations. Every prophet who has a great calling will often go through a season of great concealment. This season of being hidden prepares a prophet for the fame of being known as a man whose words never fall to the ground. This should be the desire of every called prophet.

Yet, for us to come to this place where none of our words fall to the ground, we must go through a season of impartation. Every called prophet needs an impartation of God's grace from a seasoned prophet before being released into ministry. For this to happen, we need to spend time in God's prophetic training school. We need to be in a place where the active ingredient of God's grace is imparted to our lives. Then and only then will we receive the grace we need from God so that none of our words fall to the ground.

Prophetic Extremes and False Mystiques

The School of the Prophets is a place where God's grace is released into our lives, and we are taught how to release the grace of God through our ministry into the lives of others. This is the primary purpose of prophecy: to release God's grace into the lives of God's people. When we do this, we are functioning in prophetic ministry that is profitable to God. If we do not release grace when we prophesy, then we are releasing something that is contrary to what the Father desires to release into His Son's Body.

Too often, prophets who are called but not commissioned lack this element of grace. Their words are harsh and judgmental, divisive and destructive. Most of the time, they do not even realize the damage that their words are causing within Christ's Body. This happens because they lack the spiritual wisdom and discernment necessary to see things through a balanced perspective. Their extremist views divide the Church, and everyone suffers – especially the reputation of prophets, in general.

Believe it or not, this is totally contrary to the spirit of genuine prophetic ministry. Genuine prophets are people who have learned how to live balanced lives before the Father. We can only teach others what we ourselves do. If we have not learned how to live balanced lives before the Father, we will never be able to teach others to live balanced lives before men. Because, of this, prophets should be among the most stable and dependable people in the Church.

Why then are there so many weird prophets in the Church today? Because, we have come to accept the extreme of the prophetic as normal. This has pushed the prophet and prophetic ministry to the fringes of the Church. No wonder so many pastors see prophets and prophetic ministry as an enemy of the Church. In some cases, prophets are. As the old adage says, "We have seen the enemy, and the enemy is us." This is especially true among some prophets who do weird things in the Church today.

Many contemporary prophets have unwittingly created a false mystique surrounding their ministry through marketing. I can understand why they have done this – it is hard to develop an audience in much of the Church without providing an atmosphere of entertainment. And yet, this false mystique promoted by some prophets has created false expectations among God's people regarding prophets and prophetic ministry.

We have come to view prophets and prophetic ministry through the man-made lens of powerful prophetic experiences, rather than God's visionary approach of balanced prophetic lives. This has created an unbalanced view of the prophet and his ministry within the Church. Many of the problems within the prophetic are directly related to the perceptions that we ourselves have created among people. This means that before the problems in the prophetic can be removed, our perceptions regarding prophets must change.

Do you see this? I am hopeful that what I am saying will provide the necessary impetus for prophets to change their tune and turn to a more Christ-centered approach to prophecy. My desire is to raise the standard of prophetic ministry within the Church, so that we can reach the goal of Christ for prophetic ministry: prophets who are of full stature. For this to happen, we must begin raising our attendance records and standards for today's Schools of Prophets.

Why Many Prophets Fail

Yes! There are schools for prophets today. I know of several Schools of Prophets that are being raised up right now. I believe that this is one of the greatest signs to the Church of the importance of prophets to the last day's work of God. The mere fact that God is doing this right now speaks volumes, for it shows us where we are on His timetable. The hour has come for prophets to be trained, not just in the desert as was Moses, but in a school as was Samuel.

The prophet's school is vital to the work of God. Almost all the prophets who spoke words recorded in Scripture were trained in a school for prophets as sons of the prophets. There were a few exceptions, but generally, this is how God trained His prophets for the work He called them to do. This is the ideal: Called prophets trained in the midst of a healthy prophetic community among healthy prophets who are part of the process of seeing them commissioned for the work that God has called them to do.

This is why I want to encourage all those reading this book, who know that they are called as prophets, to begin searching for Prophets' Schools. This should be the first thing a called prophet does: seek a school that will help them fulfill their calling. When we do things in God's order, we will receive things that He has for us, and be protected from the enemy's plans against us. This is where so many of God's prophets fail; they seek to go it alone. Don't fall into this trap!

I would even encourage those who have already been commissioned by Christ as prophets to seek an affiliation with a Schools of Prophets. Why? Because, there is something about being part of a larger prophetic community that adds stability and security to our lives. There is supernatural power and spiritual strength released into our lives when we find a Schools of Prophets with a like mind. When this happens, it is as if heaven opens over our lives and ministries.

Learning How to Prophesy

Why are prophetic schools so important to the development of mature prophets? Because, prophets need an atmosphere where they can be trained before they are released, an atmosphere charged with the spirit of prophecy. You can read more about how the spirit of prophecy functions in the Church today in my book on this subject entitled, *Plugging into the Spirit of Prophecy: Adding Power to Your Prophetic Words.* The spirit of prophecy will often reside in a School of the Prophets.

God deposits the spirit of prophecy into a School of the Prophets for the purpose of raising up a prophetic community. The purpose of this prophetic community is to release prophecy into the greater Body of Christ. When this happens, the spirit of prophecy can become so strong upon the School of the Prophets that even those who are not prophets can come to the school and begin prophesying (e.g., 1 Sam. 10:11-12). The spirit of prophecy can be caught, and prophets can and should be taught how to prophesy.

I know this goes against a lot of teaching in the Body of Christ, but it is nevertheless true. A prophet or prophetess needs a place to be trained to speak for God. We need to be taught how and when to minister prophetically. Although we may have a gift, we need training to use this gift to the benefit of others. As an artist needs to go to a school to refine their trade, so also a prophet should go to a prophet school to refine their skills in hearing and ministering the voice of God.

If this is true and prophets can be trained to speak prophetically, then we have no one to blame but ourselves for the mistakes that prophets make. The reason we have such shallow prophetic ministry in much of the Church is that we have spent little to no time training prophets how to prophesy. This not only contradicts what the Scriptures teach us, it is totally against good common sense. Maybe this is what we need in the prophetic today – good old common sense.

The Scriptures teach us that prophets can be taught how to prophesy. Samuel learned how to prophesy; so did Elijah, Elisha, Isaiah, Jeremiah, Ezekiel and many others. They learned how to speak the word of God to their generation by attending a school for prophets. How can I prove this? By looking closely at the Scriptures, I believe that we will see exactly what they teach us about how prophetic ministry functioned in Israel.

Samuel: Eli's Son

Let's start with Samuel. He began his prophetic ministry during the days of Eli. Samuel was born to Hannah, and lent to the Lord for service in ministry. He was born to Hannah as a result of the prophetic word that was given to her by Eli. Although it does not specifically say that it was a prophetic word, in all probability it was, because a miracle took place through that word – Samuel was born. This is when Hannah, in response to a vow she had made with the Lord, gave her son Samuel to the Lord (see 1 Sam. 1).

Think about this: Samuel grew up in the house of Eli, not Hannah. Eli became a father and mentor to Samuel. Eli trained Samuel how to hear the voice of the Lord. When the Lord began speaking to Samuel, Eli taught him how to respond to the voice of the Lord. This is what Eli taught him: he taught him to say, "Speak, Lord, for your servant is listening." How could Eli have taught this to Samuel if he himself had not first learned it? The truth is that Eli was a senior prophet, as well as priest at Shiloh in Israel.

Shiloh was a place where the people came to bring their sacrifices to the Lord. It was also a place where many people had received open visions from the Lord, prior to the priesthood of Eli. How do we know this? Because, even though the word of the Lord had become rare in Shiloh during the days of Eli, it was expected for visions to be given at Shiloh. People came to Shiloh to hear the voice of God, not just to bring their sacrifices to God.

Yet, during the days of Eli, there was no open vision, and the word of the Lord was rare. People were not hearing from God, because the prophetic ministry at Shiloh had deteriorated through Eli. In other words, they were being sent away empty-handed. God saw this, and it greatly upset Him. Yet, instead of working outside of the authority or community that He had established, God worked through it to raise up a prophet in Israel by the name of Samuel.

Elijah: Elisha's Father

What about Elijah? Elijah appears as it were from nowhere. The first time that we read about Elijah is his confrontation with Ahab. These are his first words spoken in Scripture: "As the Lord God of Israel liveth, before whom I stand, there shall not be dew nor rain these years, but according to my word." From where did Elijah come? What enabled him to speak this word to Ahab? Where did he learn how to hear the voice of God, and then turn around and speak for God to a high profile leader in Israel like Ahab?

Although the Scriptures don't tell us specifically, they do imply that Elijah attended a School of the Prophets. How do I know this? Because, he visited each major School of the Prophets before the Lord took him into heaven. This implies that Elijah was affiliated with the Schools of the Prophets in Israel, and even a leader among them. Everyone knew his name, deferred to his authority and held him in high esteem. Elijah was a prophet to the other prophets at these schools; in fact, I believe he was a senior prophet.

The Sons of the Prophets

Almost every prophet of Scripture is affiliated with a School of the Prophets. We know this because most of the prophets began their prophetic utterances similar to Isaiah's, "The vision of Isaiah, the son of Amoz..." (Is. 1:1). Why did Isaiah begin his vision this way? What was it about being the son of Amoz that was so special? In all probability, Amoz had been a well-known prophet in Israel. People knew his father, and by Isaiah saying he was the son of Amoz this lent credibility to what he prophesied.

What I would like to point out is that we don't know if Isaiah is talking about his natural father or a spiritual father who trained him to function as a prophet. More than likely it is both. Usually, the prophetic office was committed to families, not just a single person. In other words, God raised up prophets in a similar way that He raised up both priests and kings. A prophet was raised up from a prophetic family where the father trained his children how to hear and speak for God.

This is why Amos, in defending his calling as a prophet, says, "I was no prophet, neither was I a prophet's son; but I was an herdman, and a gatherer of sycamore fruit: and the Lord took me as I followed the flock, and the Lord said unto me, Go, prophesy unto My people Israel" (Amos 7:14). This means that Amos is telling us that he was an exception to the rule, not the rule. In other words, God had called him for a special purpose, and as a result, He chose to do something different in him than was normal.

This implies that the prophetic ministry and mantle should normally be passed from a prophet to his sons and daughters. A prophet's children should speak prophetically for the Lord, and have credibility in the eyes of others, because of who's son or daughter they are. This is normal and Biblical. We should think nothing of God calling whole families into the prophetic office. This was the Lord's will and way of raising up and establishing prophetic ministry in Israel, and He has established prophetic ministry this way for the past several thousand years.

I believe it is important for us to know that the oracles of God were committed to a whole prophetic community of prophetic families, not just prophetic individuals. As such, the whole family partook of the blessing of the prophetic anointing and mantle. This means that God will very often call whole families into prophetic ministry today, as He has done in the past. And this also means that the prophets who spoke for God were raised up, not as loners, but as part of a greater family and community of prophets.

This is how the Schools of the Prophets were developed: they were placed in the midst of a community of families who were called to the prophetic ministry. Children were raised up to speak the word of the Lord in the context of a greater prophetic community. This prophetic community would often minister and travel together, as they did in the days of Samuel. In fact, Samuel himself raised up several major Schools of the Prophets in his day, as did Elijah.

This is a foundational truth contained in this book on the Schools of the Prophets – God uses prophetic communities and families to raise up men and women to stand in the office of prophet. Much of the Church and many within the prophetic office today have little to no understanding of the importance of family and community to the prophetic office. I am sharing this to help you better understand the place these Schools of Prophets held in the mind of the children of Israel. When they saw these schools, they looked at them as if they were Harvard, Yale and Princeton. How completely different this view is from the way many within the Church sees prophetic ministry today!

As we continue, I will discuss several main schools that were raised up in the days of Samuel and Elijah. Although Samuel and Elijah lived at different times, they were both instrumental in leading Israel's prophetic schools: Gilgal, Bethel, Mizpeh, Ramah and Jericho. Each of these schools represents an extremely important aspect or truth that prophets need to learn for them to be able to minister effectively as prophets.

As we look more thoroughly into understanding the truth contained in these different schools, I believe God will further enlighten your understanding of the totality and completeness of genuine prophetic ministry. And, once we understand what is available to us as called prophets, we can move more freely into the fullness of God's grace upon those called into the prophetic office.

Chapter Four

What Israel's Prophet Schools Reveal

I am sometimes amazed by the fallacies based on fictional stories floating around in the Body of Christ, especially among those who are genuinely called to be prophets in the Church. We have come to believe some really strange things regarding prophetic ministry that are unscriptural and in many cases dangerous.

One of these fallacies is that prophets cannot be trained or taught how to function in the prophetic office Christ has entrusted to them. There is a sense among some prophets, believers and leaders that a prophet must learn what he learns only from God, otherwise he is not a true prophet. This has created an atmosphere of unteachability among many immature prophets who have genuinely been called by Christ. Through this false teaching, many have been lead into the lonely place of isolation, a place where they lose their ability to fulfill the calling of Christ upon their lives. How sad!

There are a great many believers who were genuinely called to be prophets that have fallen into disgrace because they lacked the proper training they should have received at a school for prophets. These individuals have never been taught how to use their spiritual gifts with wisdom to bring about an edification of the Church. Because, of this, the Body of Christ has suffered, and as a result, we have been weakened by false prophetic ministry rather than being strengthened by true prophets in our midst.

This should not be the case. The prophetic office is designed to strengthen and build-up the Body of Christ. The Church should be stronger after prophetic ministry. There should be a deposit of grace and gifts into the Church through the ministry of the prophet. This is what Paul meant when He said, "I long to see you that I may impart unto some spiritual gift to the end you may be established." The prophetic office should bring stability, security and strength to the Church.

Why then have those called to the prophetic office often done just the opposite? Because, many of them have never been trained in how to use their gifts for the benefit of the Church. This lack of training has caused prophets to become more of a source for entertainment and tickling people's ears than true spiritual advancement of the kingdom of God.

Israel's Five Prophetic Schools

Earlier, I mentioned the five Prophets' Schools in Israel. My aim in this chapter is to show you how important they were to Israel. (They were extremely important!). I want you to see with your own eyes how important these schools were to the advancement of ministry of the prophet and the kingdom of God in Israel. To do this, let's take a look at the five schools:

- Gilgal
- Bethel
- Jericho
- Mizpeh
- Ramah

I personally believe that there were more than these five schools in Israel, and yet, I believe that these particular schools reveal essential information regarding the training of those called into the ministry of the prophet. In fact, these five schools were attended and led by some of Israel's greatest prophets, including Samuel and Elijah.

Samuel was the founder of these schools, even though they were already in operation by the time he was born. Eli, his mentor and spiritual father, was a senior prophet in Israel, as well as a priest. Eli prophesied Samuel's birth and raised Samuel as his own son. There is some indication that these Schools of the Prophets go all the way back to the days of Moses when the Lord poured out His spirit of prophecy upon the 70 elders in Israel.

Why do I say that Samuel was the founder of these schools? Because, prior to Samuel, these schools weren't really tied to a location. Samuel was the first prophet in Israel to recognize the importance of developing an atmosphere of community for the prophet and his ministry to be trained and developed in Israel. This is why he raised up several schools during his lifetime, including schools for prophets at Mizpeh, Gilgal and Ramah.

These schools functioned during Samuel's lifetime and continued after his death. When we come to the days of Elijah, we see these schools still in full operation going strong. In fact, in all likelihood Elijah attended one of these schools prior to his commission as a prophet in Israel.

How do we know this? Because, later in Elijah's life, prior to his departure from earth, we see him visit several Schools of Prophets where he was respected and recognized as their leader. The schools he visited were located at Gilgal, Bethel and Jericho.

Counting the schools revealed through Samuel's and Elijah's life there are a total of five main schools for prophets in Israel: Gilgal, Bethel, Mizpeh, Ramah and Jericho. Each of these schools contains powerful principles revealing what it takes to be commissioned as a prophet. This is why I want to thoroughly understand what each of these schools meant to Israel as well as what they mean to us today. As we continue in this chapter, we will look at how these prophetic schools functioned in Israel and how they should function today. The revelation contained in understanding these schools will enable us to learn a great deal about the prophetic ministry and calling. We will see what these schools represented then, what they mean to us today and why they mean the things they do.

Gilgal: The Place of Circumcision

The school at Gilgal is the starting point for prophetic ministry. This is where prophets are trained to hear and walk under the unction of the voice of the Lord. It is a place of separation from the things in the world to the things of God. Every person called as a prophet will walk through this place of separation from the flesh to the Spirit prior to their release into the prophetic office. Without this separation from the world's system, prophets can never fulfill the call of God on their lives.

The name Gilgal literally means a circle and or wheel. The root word for Gilgal means a removing or rolling away, especially through the means of circumstances. In other words, Gilgal is a place on the potter's wheel; it is a place of shaping, forming and making. It is a place where we are circumcised and sealed into a place of covenant with God. We cut covenant with God and are brought into covenant with others. God can and does use our circumstances and relationships to change us.

There are many times where I have been on this potter's wheel of circumstance. It can be a painful process. When God begins using our circumstances to shape our lives, it hurts. We feel as if the bottom has dropped out from beneath us and wonder what we will need to do to survive. Often, we will think that we have done something wrong and that God is angry with us. He's not. He's using our circumstances to train us and separate us from the world to Himself so that we learn to depend upon His strength and not our own.

Going through this place of circumcision, cutting away of the flesh, is extremely important to the ministry of prophets. We must learn how to live in covenant with God. God deals with all of creation on the basis of covenant, and unless we learn how to live in covenant, we will end up doing more harm than good. God doesn't want this to happen. For this reason, He takes us through the place of circumcision (Gilgal) where we are placed upon the potter's wheel of life's circumstances and relationships and formed into men and women of God.

Gilgal is a place of learning how to deal with the extremities in our own hearts. It is a place where God shows us what is really on the inside of us. We see the muck and mire of the sin that is in our own hearts so that we can show others the compassion they need to be delivered from their sins. Gilgal is where we begin to see that we are sinners in need of a savior. We see the depth of the sins that are buried deep within our own hearts and as a result cry out for mercy. Every called prophet must learn to receive the mercy of the Lord before they minister for the Lord. Gilgal enables prophets to be motivated by mercy and grace so that they are able to prophesy God's true judgments from pure hearts of compassion.

Removing the Flesh

The children of Israel, prior to entering the Land of Promise during the days of Joshua, were required by God to go through a place known as Gilgal. It was in Gilgal where the children of Israel were circumcised by Joshua so that they could enter the Land of Promise. In fact, Gilgal was called the hill of foreskins in the book of Joshua; it is a place where the children of Israel left behind the foreskin of their flesh to proceed forward into the Land of Promise, a place in the Spirit.

We too must pass through Gilgal, the place of circumcision, in order for us to enter our Land of

Promise as prophets. We cannot be commissioned as prophets without first going through this place of circumcision. The place of circumcision releases us from the fleshly things that would seek to steal from us the power and presence of God. It enables us to have a heart after God, hear from God and speak for God. This is what every prophet needs prior to being commissioned.

There are three distinct circumcisions revealed in Scripture. These three circumcisions are designed by God to separate us unto Himself in three distinct areas: the heart, ears and mouth. Every prophet must have his heart, ears and mouth circumcised to the Lord so that he might be used of the Lord to minister His word from a place of wholeness to bring health to God's people.

The circumcision of the heart is the most well known of these three circumcisions, and has been used by many to represent the process we are taken through in the new birth. As this is true for a believer, so also is the true for a prophet.

A prophet must go through a place where he is reborn for the purposes of God. For some prophets, this circumcision of the heart happens at the new birth where they are simultaneously called to be prophets. For others, it happens after they have been believers for a while, and then God, according to His purposes, calls them to be prophets. Yet every prophet will go through this process of circumcision in the realm of the heart.

The Heart, Ears and Mouth

Why does God circumcise the hearts of His prophets? Because, prophets must have a heart after God. This is what made David different from Saul. David became a prophet; Saul failed to become a prophet. David has a heart after God; Saul had a heart after the world that looked to people. This is why Saul failed: he was unwilling to allow the Lord to circumcise his heart. Saul failed the test that was given to him by Lord after he had gone through Gilgal. Saul went to Gilgal, but he didn't allow the work of circumcision at Gilgal to take place in his heart. This is why Saul was among the prophets but not one of the prophets: He was unwilling to allow the Lord to circumcise his heart.

The second place of circumcision for prophets is our ears. God want to circumcise the foreskin of His prophets' ears to hear His voice. For this to happen, we need to learn how to listen to God and others. This can be extremely hard for some, especially those who are used to being the one doing the talking. Being a good listener is part and parcel to being a good prophet. A genuine prophet is a good listener; he knows how to hear God. He knows what God is saying by the sound of His voice. He can discern the voice of God because he has spent time learning how to hear His voice.

To do this, a prophet needs to discern how and what he should hear. We should not listen to everything that people tell us. The Scriptures teach us to depart from the presence of a foolish man when we don't perceive in him the lips of knowledge. Finding true wisdom among those who are speaking is a rare commodity and those who learn to listen for and to it are wise. Prophets need to learn how to do this, for wisdom is the essence of the true prophetic spirit.

Why is what prophets hear so important to their ability to be good prophets? Because, the words to which we listen shape our thinking. As people, we think about and meditate upon what we hear, even if those things are untrue. The more we listen to things that are untrue, ungodly or unhealthy, the greater the danger to our spiritual lives. As prophets, to what and to whom we listen is very important, for words can shape what we think. In fact, what and how we think about certain things can be so affected by negative words that it can damage, contaminate or prevent us from speaking the life-giving word of the Lord. When this happens, prophets are effectively silenced by the enemy and God is unable to use them to minister to His people. Do not let this happen to you. Watch what and to whom you listen as a prophet, for what and how you hear what God is saying is vital to your ability to fulfill God's calling upon your life.

The third place of circumcision is the circumcision of the mouth. Ouch! Allowing God to circumcise our mouths and tame our tongues is essential for those would like to be used in prophetic ministry. This means allowing God to cut away the things we say that are unfruitful or may be damaging to others. We cannot speak for God while at the same time presenting our own opinions. This is where many called prophets fail; they do not know when to speak and when to stay silent. In other words, they lack the diplomacy that is necessary to speak for God.

Just because we can speak prophetically to others doesn't mean that we should. God will often share with me things about others, and I will have to discern what to share and what not to share. I have learned to share only those things that are beneficial to the person listening. Why? Because, most people are not ready to hear what God is really saying. Instead, they want God to meet them on their terms. In other words, they want God to tell them what they want to hear not what they need to hear. God on the other hand tells us what we need to hear not necessarily what we want to hear. As prophets, we must learn to share what God is saying to others in a way that will draw them toward God and not push them away from Him. This is love.

Removing the Bones

As prophets, loving people means allowing God to take the painful things we say out of the way so that they can personally hear from God. I call this removing the bones from the prophetic. When we minister words that have bones of contention in them, people can choke on these bones. We don't want this to happen. Am I saying that we won't say things that cause people pain? No! What I am saying is that we need to make sure what we speak is God's word not our own. This is what being a commissioned prophet is all about: knowing how to speak the word of the Lord with circumcised lips such that we release a river of life not a swamp of death.

After going through this place of circumcision at Gilgal, the prophet will then be called into the next place of their training – Bethel.

Bethel: The Place of Revelation

Bethel is a place of divine visitation that culminates in prophetic vision and destiny. This is where prophets catch a glimpse of what God is calling them to do. Prophets are instructed by the Holy Spirit in the how's and why's of what they are called to do. God answers the deep, deep cries of their hearts by showing them the specifics of their calling as prophets. God gives His prophets these specific instructions so that they can have the necessary confidence and assurance in their hearts to fulfill His calling upon their lives.

Every prophet is called to do something specific for God. A prophet's calling is for a specific purpose. Every prophet has a specific part to play in the great drama of God's Church on planet earth. With this divine calling comes a supernatural endowment to fulfill the assigned mission and mandate. As such, every prophet is on a mission from God, and is personally responsible for fulfilling the mission or task they have been assigned. Because, of this, prophets are special in the sight of God and vital to the purpose and plan of God. God needs His prophets to fulfill the mission He has assigned them.

In Bethel, prophets learn how special they are to the heart of God. They are filled to overflowing with divine revelation and inundated with supernatural visitations of God's glory. God uses these things to impart the faith they will need to fulfill the mission for which they have been called. God nudges them into the secret place of prayer so that their hearts can be enlarged to receive all that they are able to receive. The more a prophet receives in Bethel, the more he/she has to give when they leave Bethel.

Bethel is a wonderful place for prophets. Prophets love to call Bethel their home and have a tough time leaving Bethel when God calls them to the next place. Bethel represents a place where prophets are given place and room to grow in their gifting. Prophets are given the freedom they want to pursue their destiny in God. In truth, Bethel is a mountaintop experience that few prophets want to leave. We like it at Bethel. Bethel is easy.

Abraham, while he was still Abram, went to Bethel. God visited Abram in Bethel and it radically changed his life. The Scriptures say of his visitation that Abram built an altar unto the Lord. Bethel was a place where Abram received specific answers to the prayers that he prayed. God met him at this place called Bethel in such an unusual way that he wanted to mark this spot by building an altar. In other words, he wanted to remember what God did in his life at Bethel. Prophets need to learn how to build altars of remembrance for their experiences in Bethel. This will help them when they leave Bethel and need to remind themselves of the goodness of God.

Abraham didn't stay in Bethel but left for the place God called him. Years later, there was a man, Jacob, who stumbled upon this place called Bethel. Jacob was Abraham's grandson. At this time in Jacob's life, he was running from the brother whom he betrayed. Jacob deceived Esau and stole his blessing. Esau wanted to murder Jacob for what he did. Jacob was on the run, homeless and apparently helpless. All of the tricks he used to deceive his brother backfired and reduce him to a man without a family. He had the blessing, but he lost touch with his family. He was alone.

And yet, in the midst of what must have been a low point in Jacob's life, he came into a place called Bethel, a place where his grandfather, Abraham, built an altar when he entered the Promised Land. Jacob, having stumbled upon the place of his grandfather's prayers, slept. What peace he must have felt in Bethel! While he slept, Jacob received a divine visitation from the Lord – he saw the angels of God ascending and descending from heaven. Then God spoke to him confirming His calling upon his life. Jacob became a changed man. Every prophet needs this kind of life-changing experience with God!

Prophets need Bethel. Bethel is a place of prayer, destiny, visitation, revelation and relationship. God opens prophet's eyes in Bethel and enables them to see. A prophet's eyes are opened in Bethel and he sees his calling and destiny. As a result, his faith, vision and heart are enlarged to recognize what God has called him/her to do in His house. A prophet's vision is born in Bethel. Every prophet needs God to open his/her eyes and ears in Bethel so that he/she may have the faith necessary to fulfill the call of God. A prophet's calling requires tremendous faith, vision, wisdom and compassion. Prophets receive this and more in Bethel

Bethel is where prophets learn how to connect with the Church. The name Bethel literally means house of God. Prophets learn how to rightly relate to God and others in Bethel. Prophets learn the ways of God and receive a divine revelation of God's house in Bethel. A prophet's eyes are opened in Bethel and they see that truly the Lord is in this place. In others words, prophets see that God is in His house working in the midst of His people.

When a prophet begins to see this, he will also begin seeing the value of others. Relationships become more and more important to the prophet. No longer is he a loner on the run from his brothers or sisters in the Church, but he becomes a man connected with Christ through a covenant with Christ's Church. The Church is no longer just a means to an end for the prophet to get what he wants or fulfill his calling. In truth, the Church becomes the focal point of a prophet's life's work.

When this happens, a prophet becomes married to the Church. The Church becomes an all consuming passion to the prophet. He is called to call her into covenant with Christ. The true prophet will not be desirous of Christ's bride for himself, rather he will know that she is espoused to one man, Christ Jesus. As such, the prophet will pursue the Church showing her Christ so that she will in turn pursue Him. This is the essence of what the prophet learns at Bethel.

Bethel is where a prophet learns how to walk with God in the midst of God's people, such that they are able to speak for God to His people. After all, the main purpose for the prophet is to communicate what is on the mind and heart of God to people. In Bethel, prophets are prepared by God to do this in such a way as to turn the hearts of people toward God. God uses prophets to call His people into a deeper place of intimacy and fellowship. This is what God wants from prophets and one of the main reasons why He takes His prophets to Bethel. God longs to have intimacy with His people and prophets help Him to do this.

Jericho: The Place of Consecration

Jericho is the next stop for prophets after leaving Bethel. God uses their time in Bethel to help them walk through God's training processes in Jericho.

Jericho is a hard place for prophets. In Jericho, prophets are taught how to be consecrated to the Lord. God takes the prophet through extreme situations to fully consecrate their hearts. Prophets must have the idols in their heart exposed and removed so that God can use them to do the same thing in His people's hearts. In truth, prophets learn how to lay down their life upon the altar of God at Jericho. A prophet learns to love the Lord His God with all His heart, soul, mind and strength in Jericho.

Jericho is where everything in our hearts is consecrated to the Lord. Even the seemingly small stuff of earth becomes big to God at Jericho. God will convict us on seemingly minor things in Jericho. We are brought under the Father's hand of discipline so that we do not become bastard sons who fall away and become false prophets. In Jericho, God trains us as sons so that we become fully consecrated to His purposes for His Church and people. He does this because of the great sacrifice made by His Son, Jesus.

We, as Jesus did, learn obedience to the Father in Jericho. We are tried, tested and made true prophets in Jericho, for God takes us through His school of suffering. We learn how to be consecrated to the purposes of God even in the midst of our own dire personal needs. Every genuine prophet will go through this place at some time in their life. God does this for our good to make us into the men or women that He wants us to be.

Prophets are made prophets through this period of consecration. Jericho either brings out the best or the worst in prophets. We see what is truly in our hearts, as God takes us through this consecration process. We are tried by fire and come out purer vessels more fit for the master's use. These are the processes that God takes His prophets through at Jericho.

The name Jericho literally means fragrance and is made by a combination of two root words. One of these words signifies the moon or month, and the other signifies breath or blowing upon. In other words, we could say that Jericho means a season of God blowing upon us to make us more fragrant to Himself and those around us. This means that God will, of necessity, have to remove the stench of this world from us. Parents know this time well; it is called bath time, a time where dirt is removed from our lives.

God wants to remove the dirt from our lives. It is as He removes the dirt from our lives that we become more and more consecrated to Him and His purposes. We smell less like the world and the sin in it and more like God and the fragrance of heaven. This is what God wants from His prophets: He wants us to look and smell good. Prophets cannot afford to have spiritual body odor, otherwise we can turn people away from God instead of to Him.

Being above Reproach

Prophets, of necessity, to be effective must turn people to God and not away from Him. We cannot allow even the slightest spot or stain of sin to tarnish our good reputations. In fact, we are called to have not only good reputations, but reputations that are above reproach. Others should look at our lives and see how respectably we have walked before the Lord. They should use our lives as the models for how ministers should live for God.

Think about this for a second. Prophets have a great responsibility; we are called to represent God to mankind, His Church and the world. When people see us, they should see us as ministers of God, men or women who are beyond reproach. Our lives should command the respect of those around us. Our actions should say more about God than the words that we speak. What we say will matter because people see the quality of our lives. Holy living paves the way for genuine prophetic ministry.

Doors will open to us when we live holy lives before both God and man. We cannot preach against sin on Sunday, and then live in sin on Monday. God will not tolerate this from His prophets, pastors or people. Holiness is still required to be a part of God's house. Sin can and still does disqualify people from entering into their calling in Christ. Living in sin does have consequences, even for those who are in Christ. And, in spite of what you may think or may have been taught, these consequences can sometimes be extremely severe.

The Bible declares, "It is a fearful thing to fall into the hands of the living God." And again, "Let us therefore fear lest a promise being left us of entering into His rest any of you should seem to come short of it." Or as Solomon said, "Let us hear the conclusion of the whole matter: Fear God, and keep His commandments: for this is the whole duty of man."

If these things are true for all mankind, how much more should they be true of God's prophets? We must live lives that are pleasing to God so that we can be His spokesmen. This is the crux of what prophetic ministry is all about. Jericho is an essential piece in the development of holy living in the lives of prophets. Prophets are called to tear down the things in our lives that prevent us from being consecrated wholly to the Lord. For this to happen through them, it must first happen in them. In Jericho, prophets learn to consecrate themselves to the Lord

Be Holy

When Israel went into the Land of Promise, do you remember what stronghold they faced first? It was Jericho. Jericho was a heavily fortified city surrounded by great walls designed to keep strangers out. Sin is like this; it holds people captive and prevents them from leaving the place of their captivity. Seeing this stronghold fall required a divine strategy from God. Only God can give us the weapons we need to help us overcome the sins in our own lives.

Consecration begins with revelation and brings a fortification of God's presence into our lives. For prophets to fully enter into their destiny, helping God's people enter their Promised Land, they must become consecrated to the Lord. We cannot lead God's people to where we ourselves have never been. If we want to help people overcome the sins in their lives, we must first overcome the sins in our own lives. Our consecration prepares the way for God's people to be set free from bondage to sin.

The Bible speaking about Jericho says this, "...keep yourselves from the accursed thing, lest ye make yourselves accursed, when ye take of the accursed thing, and make the camp of Israel a curse and trouble it." What is the accursed thing? The accursed thing that God is speaking of is symbolic of sin. We are to keep ourselves from sin. God teaches us to do this at Jericho. More importantly, we are taught to consecrate our lives to the Lord.

"But all the silver, and gold, and vessels of brass and iron, are consecrated unto the Lord: they shall come into the treasury of the Lord." Not everything in Jericho is to be destroyed; only those things that lead us to sin. There are redemptive natural gifts that God wants to use in our lives as prophets. God wants us to bring these things into the treasury of the Lord. Knowing the difference is what we learn at Jericho. We learn what and how to consecrate things in our lives to the Lord.

The word of the Lord to prophets at Jericho is: "Be ye holy, for I am holy."

Gilgal, Bethel and Jericho are where called prophets are transformed into commissioned prophets. God takes His called prophets through these schools for the purpose of training them to speak the word of the Lord, live sacrificial lives and walk circumspectly before men. Every called prophet is required by the Lord to go through these three Schools of the Prophets prior to being fully released into their commission.

Being commissioned as a prophet is a holy thing. God takes special care of those He commissions to stand in the office of prophet. This commission releases the necessary presence, power, provision and protection for prophets to fulfill their calling. Without this commission, a prophet's words will often fall upon deaf ears, for they will lack the conviction necessary to change hearts and minds.

Words of Power

A prophet's words when they have been commissioned will always have the power necessary to change the hearts and minds of people. God will use His prophets to speak His words to a generation that needs to hear a clear voice from heaven. A commissioned prophet's words will be heard. Their words may not be responded to immediately, yet there will be a reaction from those individuals receiving these words. A commissioned prophet's words cannot be ignored.

On the other hand, a called prophet will rarely be heard. They will often struggle in vain to get people, especially leaders, to listen to what they are saying. Their words will usually fall on deaf ears. When this happens, a called prophet can become very upset at the people or leaders who are not hearing what they are saying. Sometimes this in and of itself can be part of the process of for a called prophet to endure prior to being commissioned.

However, I suggest that we refrain from using this measurement as an acid test for determining whether a prophet is called or commissioned. Why? Because, we may be tempted, at times, to ignore a true prophets words, one who has been commissioned and sent by the Lord. I have found that people in general – especially leaders – have a tough time receiving the word of the Lord. Why? Because, it will often contradict what they themselves are thinking.

God doesn't just call His prophets to confirm what we ourselves are thinking or even what we think we have heard from the Lord. No! Prophets are called to speak the oracles of God to God's people. God calls His prophets to speak to us heaven's counsel. As such, we need to hear what prophets are saying even if we disagree or don't like what they have said. Furthermore, it is not our job to determine whether a prophet is truly commissioned (I am not saying we shouldn't test the virtue of a prophet's life or message). Our call is to simply ask the question: "Was that God?"

This is why I wrote my first book about prophecy, which was entitled *How to Know if Your Prophecy is Really from God – and What to Do if it Is*. This book establishes solid theological grounds upon which we can build our understanding of prophetic ministry. For those or you who have not read it, I would encourage you to acquire a copy of this book. It is foundational, teaching people how to receive and respond to prophets and the prophetic word.

My hope is to help prophets, especially budding prophets, identify if they themselves have truly been commissioned as a prophet by Christ. Prophets need to know this for themselves. In prophetic ministry, we cannot "fake it until we make it." If we have the true word of the Lord, people will be blessed by the words that we speak, otherwise we will only be "clouds without water, carried about of winds; trees whose fruit withereth...." In other words, we will end up in a downward spiral till we eventually crash and burn in ministry. This is not what God wants for us.

God wants His prophets to have long and fruitful lives. We are called to bear much fruit to the glory, honor and praise of His name. This means learning how to go through God's processes so that we can be fully commissioned into a place of greater authority and fruitfulness in the kingdom. And, this is what people will look for when they look at our lives; they will want to see how much fruit we have born for the kingdom. Good fruit is the primary sign of a godly commissioned prophet. As such, my prayer for everyone called and commissioned into the prophetic office is that they would bear much fruit to the glory of God. I say to all those called to prophetic ministry, "be fruitful and multiply and replenish the earth."

Chapter Five

Advanced Prophetic Training

I believe that Gilgal, Bethel and Jericho are essential for anyone called as a prophet to be commissioned into their prophetic office. Every prophet who would like to be commissioned into their calling will need to enter and graduate from these three schools. Graduation from these Prophet Schools is much like gaining a Bachelors degree in college. When we get our degree from these schools after graduation, we are then commissioned to use our abilities to help the Body of Christ. This should happen with the blessing of the senior prophet and his staff through prophetic ministry, charging the newly commissioned prophet into their calling. When this happens, God will begin opening doors to us so we can fulfill the commission He has given to us. Divine order in a prophet's life sets the stage for divine connections.

However, this is just the beginning of being trained if a commissioned prophet wants to move further in his or her ministry. In this chapter, we will take look at the advanced courses available to commissioned prophets. We can find these advanced courses by looking at the final two Schools of the Prophets: Mizpeh and Ramah. I like to think of these two schools as Masters and Doctorate schools of prophetic ministry. In other words, we will learn things in Mizpeh and Ramah that will bring us into a higher realm in the prophetic than what we have already learned at Gilgal, Bethel and Jericho.

Knowing there is more available is important for prophets to grasp. It can be easy for prophets to think that they have arrived when, in reality, they have only taken the first step toward the fulfillment of their destiny. We can always learn more, and God will always show us more, if we are willing to pay the price to go to a higher, wider, deeper place in Him. Not every prophet will be called to Mizpeh or Ramah. However, those who are called into these schools will gain valuable revelation concerning God's prophetic ways as well as an increase in the prophetic flow through their lives.

Prophets to Nations

Advanced prophetic training isn't for every prophet. Most prophets can fulfill their calling without going through what Mizpeh and Ramah represent. God calls very few to Mizpeh and fewer still to Ramah. Those who are called to these schools of higher learning in prophetic ministry are being prepared for something extraordinary – becoming prophets to nations and/or senior prophets. Both require advanced training in prophetic ministry.

God calls certain prophets to be prophets to nations. Jeremiah was called by God to be a prophet to nations. Listen to what the Scripture says about the calling of Jeremiah, "See, I have this day set thee over the nations and over the kingdoms, to root out, and to pull down, and to destroy, and to throw down, to build and to plant" (Jer. 1:10). Jeremiah was called to be a prophet to nations, and God set him over kingdoms.

Prophets called to nations are rare exceptions. God doesn't call every prophet to nations. Even those prophets who have national or international ministries may not be prophets to nations. A prophet to nations has been set by God over a particular people group or nation for the purpose of bringing His rule through the prophetic word. Prophets to nations will typically have access to top officials in governments, and the words they speak will be so strong that governments will not be able to overlook what they say.

When a prophet called to a specific nation or nations speaks, people within the nation to which they are called to speak will not be able to avoid what they say. God will use their words to pierce through the wall of separation between Church and state bringing God's government into the nations to which they are called. Their words will become the vehicle through which God begins exercising His authority over nations bringing blessing or judgment.

History records many prophets called to nations. One such prophet was a man by the name of John Knox. Mary, Queen of Scots, said this of him, "I fear the prayers of John Knox more than the armies of England." What a statement! Can you see the authority this man exercised over this nation through his words and prayers? God used him as a prophet to this nation, holding its leadership accountable for their actions.

God has not changed His ways, He still rules the nations. Jeremiah was called to nations, plural. John Knox was called to a nation, singular. God still calls individuals to be prophets to a single nation or multiple nations. In a future book, I plan to teach about the calling on prophets to the nations. I will do this to help believers, Church leaders and her prophets understand the nature of prophets to the nations. I will do this to help bring clarity of understanding to an area where there has been much confusion by many within the Church.

We need to understand the calling upon prophets to nations for God is still seeking to use them today. In this current book and in future books, I will seek to bring further understanding regarding the specific details of the calling and commissioning of prophets to nations. Yet, for now, it is important for us to see why there is a need for advanced prophetic ministry training. I hope you see this through what I have written so far. Those prophets called to the nations or called to be senior prophets need additional training to fulfill the prophetic calling upon their lives. This is the crux of this chapter where I detail the training available to prophets through the Schools of Prophets at Mizpeh and Ramah.

Mizpeh: The Place of Warfare Prayer

Prophets to nations require additional training to fulfill their calling. A prophet to nations will not be able to handle what comes their way if they have only gone through the training process of Gilgal, Bethel and Jericho. For an individual to fulfill their ministry calling as a prophet to nations, they will, of necessity, need what God will teach them in their time of advanced prophetic training. This means they will need something more than they already have, they will need what can only come at a place called Mizpeh.

The Scriptures do not say too much about this School of Prophets beyond the fact that Samuel visited this place every year, as he did in Gilgal and Bethel. Because, of this, we can infer that a Schools of Prophets was in fact at Mizpeh, even though the Scriptures don't tell us this for sure. What we do see, however, is the importance Mizpeh held in the mind of Samuel. Samuel won a great victory at Mizpeh. He also judged all Israel at Mizpeh. Doesn't it make sense that he would also train prophets in Mizpeh while he stayed there?

I think so little is said about Mizpeh because of it's place of importance in the training of prophets to nations. God has a special place in His hearts for prophets, especially those prophets He calls to nations. A prophet to nations will go through a different and more difficult degree of training than other prophets. Why? Because, they will be held to a higher standard of accountability before both God and man. This higher standard of accountability comes because their words have the ability to impact entire nations and people groups.

God does not treat it lightly when a prophet speaks something that He Himself has not spoken. If a prophet to nations speaks a word that is not from the mouth of the Lord, the discipline upon that prophet can be severe, even deadly. This is why prophets to nations go through a more severe training process than prophets to the Church. The severity of the training reveals the authority of the calling. The more severe the training, the greater the calling and authority given to that particular prophet.

A prophet to nations has the ability to affect the course of whole people groups. The history of nations can change through the words of prophets to nations. When a prophet to nations speaks, their words can turn once prosperous nations into barren wastelands. Miracles, signs and wonders will often follow the words they speak. Their words can open or close heaven. They can issue judgments or blessings based upon what God reveals to them. Often, there is little difference between what they see and what God sees. This is just a sample of what happens when prophets to nations speak.

Because, prophets to nations wield this level of authority, their training is usually more severe. God thoroughly trains those He calls as prophets to nations. He takes them to Mizpeh so they can receive the additional training they need to stand in their calling as prophets to nations. Knowing these things can aid prophets to nations, so they don't spend years wandering in the desert, outside of the will of God, waiting to enter into their calling to the nations.

In order to illustrate what I am saying, I would like to share a story that Kenneth Hagin, Sr. shared about himself and something the Lord told him that radically changed his ministry. As he told the story, there was a point in his life where he felt like he was washing his feet with his socks on. In other words, something just didn't feel right about what he was doing. Over the next few months, he began seriously seeking the Lord. One day he received a vision. In this vision, the Lord showed him what he needed to do to enter the next phase of his ministry. Then, according to Hagin, the Lord made this startling statement: Most ministers never enter into the fullness of their calling.

Think about this for a second. Isn't this shocking? And yet, I believe it is true. The question is: "Why does this happen?" I believe the answer is simple: Most ministers miss what God has prepared for them because they never receive the necessary training to move to the next level. Kenneth Hagin Sr. would have missed God had he not been willing to listen to this inner voice telling him that something was wrong in his ministry. Instead he listened and sought the Lord, receiving the revelation he needed to move forward in ministry. Today, because he was willing to be obedient to what the Lord told him, millions have been touched by his ministry.

God desires for us to be obedient to Him in our calling as ministers like Kenneth Hagin Sr. We should consistently be moving forward in our calling. To do this, we need to go through the necessary preparation process. God always uses processes of preparation to promote us in His kingdom. The Scripture says, "Promotion doesn't come from the east or the west promotion comes from the Lord." This is especially true for those called as prophets to nations. God alone can promote His prophets to this place of honor.

Being a Intercessory Watchman

Prophets to nations are prepared for ministry through the training processes that take place at Mizpeh. Although God may call a man or woman to a nation, He will not commission them until they have been fully trained. Their gift may make room for them, but their words will not be effectual in bringing the change necessary for God's will to be accomplished until they are commissioned by the Lord. Learning how to speak the right word from the Lord at the right time to bring the right results takes years of training. This happens at Mizpeh.

At Mizpeh, prophets learn how to wait to speak the word of the Lord. They learn how to observe what God is doing, what people are doing and what the enemy is doing. The name Mizpeh in

Hebrew literally means watchtower. In other words, prophets while at Mizpeh learn how to wait to speak the word of the Lord at the right time and in the right way. God establishes boundaries of what to say, when to say it and how it should be said. Prophets learn all this and more at Mizpeh.

Mizpeh is a place of deep intercession. While prophets are at Mizpeh, they will often lose themselves in the secret place of prayer. Prayer will become their reason for living. Everything they do will be identified by prayer. They will do nothing without effectual fervent prayer. Their hearts will reach out to people in obedient intercession, longing to see the will of God done in the nation or nations to which they are called. This is what prophets learn at Mizpeh; they learn how to care for people through prayer.

The more a prophet cares for the people they are called to, the more they will pray for these people. God calls prophets as prophets to nations because they have chosen to love others through their prayers of intercession. They will literally war over people against principalities and powers until people are set free. They stand in the gap saying to the principalities and power, "Let my people go!" The yearning in their hearts is for people to be free. Prophets to nations are looking to free people from the dictates of sin so they can surrender to God.

Sometimes, prophets to nations can become so involved in prayer for people that they can overstep the boundaries of their calling. This is one of the things prophets to nations need to learn how to avoid. God calls His prophets to pray for people through fervent intercession, and yet, sometimes this is not enough. When this happens, often prophets will be called to give people over to their sin and the judgment that this sin brings. This can be very difficult because the prophet has a heart for the people that has been cultivated through prayer. A prophet's heart for people can lead him astray if he does not keep his heart in check. Mercy is not mercy if it does not originate in the heart of God. God is much greater than we are, and He is perfectly just and compassionate at the same time. As prophets to nations, we are called to trust in the God at these moments.

Mature prophets understand that God's temporary judgment upon sin can be far better for nations, or people, than their perpetual deterioration into sin. When prophets begin to hold back the judgment of God through prayer, this can prevent people from learning to fear the Lord. The Bible declares, "When your judgments are in the world the inhabitants thereof will learn righteousness." In other words, some things will never be learned unless we begin to see the judgments of God in the earth.

This is a real problem in among many of the prophets in the Church today. Prophets today can be squeamish about pronouncing God's judgments upon nations for sin. Some prophetic leaders have even come to believe that it is wrong to do this. Other prophetic leaders will not listen to prophetic declarations of judgment unless there is a corresponding call to prayer. Prophets have slipped in their calling, and people continue to slip deeper and deeper into sin because prophets have not gone through the necessary preparation at Mizpeh.

Praying for Mercy or Judgement

Mizpeh changes our perspective regarding the ways of God. While in Mizpeh, we learn that the judgments of God can be a good thing. We see beyond our temporal perspective and start to view things through a timeless perspective. As such, we catch a glimpse of what God must see from His eternal perspective. Instead of instantly calling for mercy, we start to see judgment as a better option at particular times and seasons. We can only see things from this perspective as we see the ravaging effects of sin over the course time, sometimes generations.

The Bible declares, "The wages of sin is death." Sin always brings death and destruction into the lives of people. Because, of this, there are times when the judgments of God upon a society may be better than the wages of sin. Sin always dulls the conscience of man. Eventually sin can become so sinful that we are given over to it. When this happens, this can spell certain doom and the end of a civilization. Prophets to nations see this, and as such, will speak prophetically to turn people from their sin. Sometimes this requires prophetic declarations of judgment by the prophet.

Can you see what I am saying? Prophets to nations must come to the point where they can issue God's judgments without respect of persons. Then and only then, can they bring the nations to which they are called into a place of righteousness before God. Prophets to nations can even come to the place where they see the judgments of God through God's light, as David did. Listen to what David said regarding the judgments of God, "More to be desired are they than gold, yea than much fine gold: sweeter also than honey and the honeycomb" (Ps. 19:10). This is how prophets view the judgments of God after they have gone through the preparation process at Mizpeh.

Does this mean every prophet calling for the judgments of God is speaking from the mouth of the Lord? Hardly! Quite often, prophets who are very immature will speak forth judgments upon situations or people not realizing what they are doing. I call this the baby stage of being a prophet. Many prophets in their baby stages will pronounce judgments on everything from the mail system to the government to Church leaders and so on. Their immaturity can create many messes which need to be cleaned up. At this stage, diapers are not a bad thing.

There is a difference between the two. One has years of maturation under their belt. They have gone through hell to catch a glimpse of what heaven is saying. They have seen the world and tasted of it's suffering, and as a result, have learned how to show compassion toward others. The other has little to no experience with trials, tribulation or suffering. They speak from their own hearts what they think God is saying rather than truly hearing the voice of the Lord. Here is where judging a prophet by the fruit of their lives becomes a vital part in our ability to discern the maturity of the prophet.

Performance vs. Character

Understanding the differences between these two types of individuals is extremely important. One has earned the right to be heard. Their life experiences have prepared them to speak for God in the areas of judgment. The other is seeking to earn this right through the accuracy of the words they speak. Prophets do not earn the right to be heard through the accuracy of their words. Instead, it is their quality of character gained in the fiery trials of God's processes that prepare them to speak words of judgment and earn them the right to be heard by today's leaders.

In other words, we should listen to those prophets who have been to the watchtower and seen things from the place of years of experience and intercession. These have earned the right to be heard by battling against the enemy through their prayers and words to hold back darkness over nations. God has taught them at Mizpeh and commissioned them to be prophets to nations. The other is still in diapers looking to enter into their calling as prophets. They still have not even entered the Schools of Prophets. Do you see the difference?

Why am I saying all this? Because, inevitably there will be those who will twist what I am saying to make themselves appear to be mature prophets. In reality, those who need this kind of recognition are still babes in the prophetic. Knowing the difference between these two is especially important for leaders. I am pointing out the differences in hopes of helping leaders and believers hear those who have the right to be heard. We need prophets in our midst who have earned the right to be heard. We need them to speak the word of the Lord, including words of judgment. We need this for the Church's sake so that we are not caught off guard or totally given over to sin. Amen.

Mizpeh prepares prophets to speak for the Lord through the vehicle of intercession and judgment, calling for war against the powers and principalities or sins that holds nations in bondage. Thank God for prophets who have paid the price to speak for God to nations. May God use this and my upcoming book on prophets to nations to help raise up a host of prophets to nations for the end times.

Ramah: The Place of Spiritual Parenting

After Mizpeh, some prophets are called further into the depths of prophetic ministry to a place known as Ramah. Ramah is for prophets who have been called to be fathering or mothering prophets or what some would term apostolic prophets. Becoming a senior prophet doesn't happen overnight. With a senior prophet's calling to train others in prophetic ministry comes a tremendous responsibility. Senior prophets are responsible for leaving behind a healthy legacy of prophetic ministry for future generations.

A senior prophet is vital to God's plan for nations and generations. When God calls a man or woman to be a senior prophet, they will go through circumstances designed to break them of self will and reveal to them God's will. God will mold their will to be like His so that He can use these prophets to raise up others like them in the ministry to which He has called them. God uses senior prophets to reproduce the seed of prophetic ministry in the lives of other for future generations. This is the calling upon the life of a senior prophet.

Every ministry gift has fathers who are called to reproduce what God has done in and through them. Evangelists have fathers in ministry, as do pastors and teachers. Apostles are usually trained at the feet of another apostle, like Timothy was with Paul. Spiritual fathers are rare, for as Paul says, "Ye have not many fathers." Fathering prophets are a rare gift from God to the Church. As such, they need to be recognized for what they are called to do.

Senior prophets do something other prophets are not able to do, they raise up men and women with a heart for prophetic ministry. Fathering prophets seek the best for their sons. They will look to promote the ministry of their children rather than their own ministry. Instead of having students, they will have sons. In fact, the Schools of the Prophets were usually called sons of the prophets. This signifies the kind of relationship senior prophets have with their students, they see them as sons.

Senior prophets have Schools of Prophets for the purpose of perpetuating the ministry of the prophet. Elijah was a senior prophet, so was Samuel, Elisha, Deborah and Micah. All of these men stood as senior prophets to their generation. They raised up solid prophetic ministries for generations to come. Many of the prophets in Israel came from these Schools of Prophets. The

111

Church today owe a great debt to the men and women God used as senior prophets in Israel. And, we need these same kinds of senior prophets in our day.

The Price of Being a Spiritual Parent

Becoming a senior prophet comes at a great price. Ramah tells us the price of being a senior prophet. Samuel dwelt in Ramah, as did Deborah. Both were used mightily as senior prophets. Jeremiah says this about Ramah, "In Ramah there was a voice heard Rachel weeping for her children..." In other words, in Ramah a cry is born in the heart of senior prophets so they can birth prophetic sons and daughters. This is why Samuel wept so much over Saul; he wanted Saul to fulfill his calling.

Ramah is a place of weeping. It is a place where senior prophets are made tender toward emerging prophets. God calls senior prophets to weep over their sons and daughters, helping them find their calling in Christ so they can fulfill their destiny as prophets. A senior prophet may spend years travailing over their sons and daughters for the purpose of bringing forth God's will through them. They will spend their lives leaving behind a godly prophetic legacy. This will be the focus of their ministry.

Senior prophets look to the interests of their sons and daughters. Their relationship with their sons and daughters is built on the trust that has come through the time they have spent with them. Often, senior prophets will give their sons and daughters on the job training. What do I mean by this? I mean spiritual sons and daughters will learn how to minister prophetically as they serve the senior prophet in ministry. This has been called by some, "holding another man's coat." Senior prophets will often train their sons and daughters this way.

Holding another man's coat in the kingdom of God is a good thing if it is done the right way. There are many who claim to be spiritual fathers and mothers who have little concern for their supposed spiritual sons or daughters. Instead, they use the title of spiritual father or mother to promote their abusive control over the lives of naive individuals called to ministry. God abhors this type of control in leadership, especially among those who are truly called to be spiritual fathers or mothers.

Spiritual Fathers and Mothers

Getting a good deal on low-priced help is not God's way of building His kingdom. Using spiritual sons and daughter as beasts of burden is not God's will. Building our own kingdom on the backs of unsuspecting individuals is not God's way. Our Father would never think of using or abusing His children this way. No! Being a spiritual father or mother does not give us the right to use our spiritual sons or daughters as stepping stones to further our own ministries. This is of the world, the flesh and ultimately the devil.

No! A genuine spiritual father or mother would never seek to do things this way. Instead, they look for opportunities to promote their spiritual sons and daughters in ministry. Spiritual fathers and mothers look for practical ways to help their spiritual sons and daughters grow in ministry by providing them with contacts, references or other tangible means of support. Remember God's way is that the elder lay up for the younger. At least, this is what the Scriptures teach.

Providing for the next generation is extremely important to God. God longs for men and women of God to step into the place of becoming spiritual fathers and mothers. Being a spiritual father or mother is hard work, and is not something to be attempted by the timid, selfish or prideful. This is what parenting is always about laying up, giving out and providing for. Spiritual fathers and mothers always seek to make room for their spiritual sons and daughters, thereby making it easier for them to succeed in ministry.

This is the nature of parenthood, whether in the natural or spiritual. God gives us parents, for our good, to help provide for and protect us while we are in this world. The world is a complex and dangerous place, and it can be difficult, if not impossible, to navigate on our own. This is why we need parents. God has provided parents as a shield of protection from the harm enemies in the world would seek to do us.

Parents are designed by God to protect their children. The proverbs say this about mothers, "Let a bear robbed of her whelps meet a man, rather than a fool in his folly." By implication, the writer is telling us that a female bear robbed of her children can be a dangerous creature. None of us would want to meet a mama bear in this kind of situation, would we? If this is true of animals and their parenting skills, how much more has

God instilled this nature in us – the crown of His creation?

Parenting is an art. Learning how to understand and train spiritual sons or daughters does not come easily. All children by nature want their own way. Parents by nature are called to help their children understand which way to go. This can and will create conflict at some level in their relationship, always. However, if a spiritual parent understands how to teach their spiritual children by example, this conflict can be lessened, and an appreciation can develop in the hearts of spiritual children for their spiritual parents. This should be our goal in being spiritual parents.

Spiritual parents are called to mentor those under their care. We are to fully bring our sons and daughters into their destiny. God wants all those He calls to ministry to fulfill their calling. Many individuals never enter into their full calling. According to Kenneth Hagin Sr., a well respected leader, the Lord spoke to him in a vision and most ministers never complete even the first level in their assignment what an indictment against us! We must change so that this doesn't happen in our lives or the lives of our spiritual children.

How can we do this? By learning how to become better spiritual parents. I believe that every senior prophet needs their own personal Ramah experience, an experience where their hearts are turned to the next generation. They need this kind of an experience to learn how to become a spiritual father or mother. A generation of Elishas needs a generation of Elijahs to train and raise them into their purpose and place in God. This will only happen if, and when, senior prophets have their heart turned to the next generation. Only then will the children's heart be turned toward spiritual fathers and mothers and not away from them.

Patience, Perseverance and Persistence

This is what Ramah is designed to do in the life of a senior prophet, give them a glimpse into the Fathering heart of God. When senior prophets come to this place where their own hearts are turned to the Father, they will then be ready to mentor coming generations of prophets. This will cause senior prophets to be lifted up in the eyes of their spiritual children so their children can receive all senior prophets have to impart to them. Being able to do this requires patience, persistence and fortitude. A senior prophet must be able to see their children as God has called them to be so that they will not be tempted to give up on them when the going gets tough. Every spiritual parent will endure a spiritual child's temper tantrums. A true father or mother knows when and how to discipline a true son or daughter in the faith.

When God brings a spiritual parent into a person's life, quite often the person does not immediately recognize it. They will very often be oblivious to the fact that a mentor has entered their life. And yet, over the process of time, as spiritual parents pour their lives into the lives of sons and daughters, their children become ready and willing to learn.

This does not mean that every spiritual son or daughter will receive their spiritual parent – they may not. There are times where spiritual children will reject their spiritual parents. This happened to Paul, John and other apostles in the Early Church. It will happen to us if we are called to be spiritual parents. However, those who receive the benefit of our years of experience will receive the blessing associated with this experience of God's anointing, power and presence. Furthermore, their personal lives will be impacted by the tender touch of our years of experience as we patiently guide them into the Father's hands. This requires patience and persistence on the part of the parent.

In truth, I believe the primary characteristic of every genuine spiritual parent is patience. An impatient person can never be used by God as a spiritual parent. Paul, in writing to his children in the faith said, "Truly the signs of an apostle were wrought among you in all patience..." Patience was Paul's key as a spiritual parent. He used this key to open the hearts of his sons and daughters in the faith. The same will be true of those called to be senior prophets.

Chapter Six

Raising Up Prophetic Families

Understanding the prophetic call is vital to our understanding of the prophetic office. As I have previously said, prophets are made not born. Although the calling may be given at birth, prophets will not usually begin fulfilling this calling until they have gone through the necessary preparation through training. We have looked at this training process over the last couple chapters. I have wanted to paint a clear picture of how God works in the lives of prophets to prepare them to do His work.

My understanding of prophets being prepared for ministry involves God training them at schools for prophets. These schools are instrumental in teaching prophets how to flow with the Holy Spirit. As prophets learn to flow with the Holy Spirit, they can then begin to function in the prophetic office. As such, I believe that prophets are made prophets through schooling, learning and training. Everyone called into prophetic office will go through this training process, either in a school for prophets or in the school of hard knocks. I believe it is much easier for the prophet if they choose a School of the Prophets.

Does this mean that Prophet Schools have always been in the Church as they should be? Hardly! Prophets have many times gone through their training in what some have termed a desert experience. This desert experience is designed by God to empty the prophet of himself so that he can be filled with the Holy Spirit of prophecy. As this happens, the prophet learns how, when and where to speak the words of God. A prophet can learn this through a time in the desert, as many have, or in a Schools of Prophets. Both are equally viable for training prophets, however, being trained for prophetic ministry in a school for prophets is usually far easier than wandering through a desert type experience. I have experienced both and preferred my time in school as opposed to my time in the desert.

What I want you to understand is this: All prophets go through training, but not all prophets are trained in the same way or place. Because, we have not understood the prophetic office, or how God trains prophets to function in ministry, we have made some incorrect assumptions. I have sought to debunk some of these inaccurate underlying assumptions through my writings in this book, as well as in my two previous books on prophecy. I have done this to bring clarity of understanding regarding prophets and prophetic ministry into the minds of prophets, leaders and believers within the Church. I hope this has been helpful in your understanding of prophets.

My desire has been to not repeat what others authors have already written on prophets and prophecy. I have read many of the books that are available on prophets and prophecy. Some, I have found to be very good, and others, I have found to be very bad. Most have dealt with specific issues concerning prophets and prophecy that were important at the time the authors wrote their books. I have listed several resource books I believe to be on the cutting edge of what God is saying about prophets and prophecy in the back of this book.

A Transgenerational Call

As we seek to understand prophets and define how prophetic ministry should function in the Church, I believe it is important for us to review God's process in raising up ministers. Once we do this, we can better understand how God calls, anoints and appoints prophets to speak for Him. This is what I will seek to bring through effective teaching into this chapter. I want to help us better understand God's process for establishing prophets in the Church.

To do this, I believe it is imperative that we have a basic understanding of the calling to the prophetic office. Every ministerial calling is vital to the Church, whether that of a prophet, pastor or preacher. Every called minister has been set by God into the place where they now stand. Being called into ministry is essential for every ministry gift. Knowing God has called someone into the ministry is a sure foundation upon which their calling can be established. This foundation will help someone called into ministry run the race set before them with patience. It will also provide them with purpose as men and women of God.

A prophet's call is vital to the foundation of his ministry. Without knowing we have been called into the prophetic office, we will always question whether or not our ministry is valid in the Church. As such, we need to identify and understand the ways God calls His prophets into this vital ministry.

Many prophets and leaders have focused upon their personal calling by God, and how God spoke to them about that calling. That is not what I want to do in this chapter. What I would like to do is offer some explanation as to how and why prophets are usually called within the sphere of a prophetic family. In other words, prophets are usually called on the basis of their family lineage. The prophetic calling is usually transgenerational in nature, as are many of the other callings in ministry.

Our Father in heaven is family minded. God created the family structure, and He has chosen to work in and through families throughout all of history. Even today, when we look at how individuals choose their profession, very often they choose to walk in the steps of their father or mother. This is why being the son of a prophet in Scripture is such an important statement. God usually calls His prophets in the context of prophetic families.

Why is understanding this truth about the prophetic office so important? For the simple reason that, as we come to understand the basic calling into prophetic ministry, we can begin seeing how this calling is functioning in the Church today. Once we see how it is functioning in the Church today, we can come along side prophets and begin to support them. Supporting prophets and prophetic ministry in the Church is vital to a prophet's ability to fulfill their calling to the Church. And in the process receive the blessing associated with supporting the prophet and his ministry.

The Prophet's Reward

Prophecy and blessing go hand in hand. When a prophet speaks prophetically into our lives, they are speaking a blessing from God over us. To receive a prophet's blessing is essential to our spiritual growth as individuals and churches. There is power resident in the blessing of a true prophet or prophetess. Jesus said, "He who receives a prophet in the name of a prophet will receive a prophet's reward."

Think about this for a second. This is a powerful statement from Christ himself. Jesus, the Son of God, is clearly calling us to support prophets and prophetic ministry. Why does He want us to do this? So we can receive the blessing a prophet brings into our lives. There is no other statement like this in the Bible regarding any of the other ministry gifts. Here Jesus is telling us that there are tangible rewards given to those who support prophets. God has placed a tangible blessing upon the lives of prophets, and we can receive this blessing by supporting what God has called them to do.

Supporting prophets is an important part of creating an environment that is healthy for prophets in the Church. When there is a lack of support for prophets by the Church, the enemy is able to plant false prophets in the Church. As such, how we support prophets will determine the quality of the prophetic word in our midst. This is why God uses spiritual fathers and mothers as a conduit whereby emerging prophetic ministries can be supported.

Spiritual fathers and mothers are important to healthy prophetic ministry. When called prophets are nurtured by mature senior prophets, the Body of Christ greatly benefits from the spiritual sons and daughters reproduced. God designed all of creation this way. We reproduce after our own kind. The spiritual DNA of prophets is often determined by the spiritual fathers and mothers who trained them.

Spiritual DNA and Inheritance

An impartation of spiritual DNA will often takes place at the Schools of Prophets. Senior prophets will have a direct bearing upon the quality of prophetic ministry reproduced in the Church. And yet, senior prophets are only one vehicle God uses to impart spiritual DNA to emerging prophets. Therefore, we cannot assume that senior prophets are the only ones who can impart prophetic DNA. I believe this would be an incorrect assumption and violate the core of what the Scriptures teach about how God raise up prophets. The Scriptures teach clearly that, most of the time, prophetic DNA is imparted through actual natural fathers and mothers of prophets.

The Bible is replete with instances where whole families were called by God for specific places of ministry. For example, Noah had three sons Shem, Ham and Japheth. God saved Noah's three sons because they were Noah's sons. God blessed them and renewed his calling upon all mankind through them. God called Noah's entire family to survive the flood, not just Noah. Families do matter to God.

Another example of God blessing families is Abraham. Abraham and his family were called, anointed and blessed by God. God blessed Isaac because he was the son of his father, Abraham. Even before Isaac was born, God had promised to Abraham that "in Isaac shall your seed be called." Isaac did nothing to merit God's blessing beyond being born. It wasn't the faith of Isaac that cause this blessing, but the faith of Abraham. Abraham prepared the way, through faith, for his son, Isaac, to be blessed. What an example for fathers to follow. Families and fathers do matter to God.

To illustrate this point even further, look at Moses, Miriam and Aaron. God truly blessed this family. All of these Biblical figures were ordained by God as prophets. The Bible speaking of Moses says, "My servant Moses... With him I will speak mouth to mouth, even apparently, and not in dark speeches..." God called Moses as His prophet, and He called Aaron as Moses' prophet. The Scriptures speaking about this say, "And he shall be thy spokesman unto the people: and he shall be, even he shall be to thee instead of a mouth, and thou shalt be to him instead of God."

131

Miriam was included in the prophetic calling upon this family, for the word of God says of her, "And Miriam, the prophetess the sister of Aaron, took a timbrel in her hand and all the women went out after her with timbrels and dances." Do you see how important families are to God?

Born into a Calling

This is how God works – He works through families. Why am I saying this? Because, I want you to see that God doesn't just call individuals, He often calls entire families. This is especially true for prophets. Prophets are usually part of prophetic families who are called by God to fulfill certain functions within the Church. God rarely calls individuals alone; He usually calls entire families to fulfill a calling within the Church. Why does God do this? Because, He delights in raising up families to fulfill specific areas of ministry. We need to be cognizant of this reality as we move forward in our understanding of prophets and prophetic ministry.

When God raised up the priesthood, for example, He raised up the priests according to families. So also prophets were usually part of prophetic families. Prophetic families would then gather into a larger prophetic community whereby prophets could be trained and commissioned for ministry. As such, the prophetic office and word was passed from one generation to another. This was and is God's way for raising up prophets. God likes to raise up prophets in the midst of prophetic families for the purpose of bringing continuity to the prophetic calling upon the family.

God doesn't just call individuals, He calls families. As such, every member of the family partakes of the calling and anointing of God. This means our destiny in life is often linked to our family lineage. We can easily see this in the natural with musical families, sports families or political families. The people who are part of these families will often enter into the same arena as their fathers or mothers. In some cases, they will be better or worse at particular areas of these callings.

Most people have heard of the Jackson family. Can you imagine growing up in this family without begin musically inclined? Hard to imagine, isn't it? When we think of the Jackson family, we think of their music. In fact, it would be hard to talk about the Jackson family without talking about their music. In truth, this is part of who they are and who God made them to be. It is easy to recognize the calling upon this family because it is so evident. They are a musical family.

The Kennedy family is also a famous family with a unique calling. Most of us are able to recognize this calling immediately as leadership. We see the great leaders that have come from the Kennedy family and wonder who else will be raised up from that family. America and the world have been fascinated by this family because of their unique quality of leadership. It is hard to not identify the calling upon this family because it is so visible.

Another family most of us would recognize is Graham family. When we think of this family, we think of great ministers. Billy Graham is a preacher of preachers who has gained recognition around the world. It is hard to imagine a world without him or his family. And, it is easy to recognize the calling of God upon this family. To deny the calling upon this family would be ridiculous to most of us. We recognize the calling and anointing that God has placed upon this family, a calling to minister the gospel of God through evangelism.

A Healthy Model for Prophetic Ministry

The same is true for prophets and prophetic families. God raises up His prophets in the context of prophetic families. This is the normal way for prophets to grow in their gifts and callings in God. Prophet will usually learn how to prophesy through prophetic parents. The way God speaks to the parents is often the way He speaks to the children. Prophets who have visions will often have children who have vision. Prophets who have dreams will often have children who have dreams. Prophets who hear the audible or inward voice of God will often have children who hear God's audible or inward voice. These are God's ways for raising up prophets.

Why is it important for us to understand that prophets are raised up in the context of prophetic families? Because, this cuts clear against the grain of the thinking presently in the Church regarding prophets. Many have seen prophets as loners, unable to relate to anyone under any circumstances. And, while some prophets may have fit this profile, most will not be this way. Furthermore, if this is the stereotype we use to look for prophets, we will look for unhealthy role models to guide us in prophetic ministry.

135

Therefore, it is vital that we determine the true nature of the prophetic ministry. This is why I have sought to develop and lay a foundation for understanding how prophets are trained. When we look for prophets, we should see these tell tale signs of prophetic training in their lives. This doesn't mean that every prophet will go through the exact same training process the same way, but it does give us clues as to what to look for in identifying true prophets.

Additionally, as long as our perspective of prophets in the Church is skewed, we will inevitably search for prophets who are not healthy role models for ministry. And, this will further distance prophets from the rest of the Church. This would not be a good thing for prophets or for the Church. Prophets and church leaders must learn how to relate to one another. For this to happen, church leaders must learn to identify the blessing prophets bring to the church and prophets must learn how to relate in acceptable ways within the greater context of the church by learning to work with and not against church leaders.

So then, understanding how God raises and trains prophets is vital to learning more about the nature and ministry of the prophet. If prophets are raised in healthy prophetic families, first, and then trained in schools for prophets, second, as I am presenting in this book, we will see the prophetic ministry move forward into its full purpose in God: the furthering of the kingdom of God through prophetic ministry. This is what we want.

Maturing His Body, Preparing His Bride

Prophecy is good for the growth of God's kingdom. As such, prophets help the kingdom of God to grow into every part of the earth. For this reason prophets and prophecy are valuable to church leaders. When we see prophets through this light, we begin to recognize their importance to the church. Prophets are important to the church, for they help the church grow into the image of God's Son, our Lord and Savior, Jesus Christ. Church leaders should want this for everyone in the church.

For the church to come to the place of her calling in Christ, she will need to learn how to receive and place an importance upon prophets and prophetic ministry. If we are to become the bride of Christ, we will need to have every spot and wrinkle of the world removed from our lives. How does this happen? Certainly, one of the primary ways this happens is as prophets speak prophetically to the church, washing her with the water of Christ's word.

Praise God for prophets and prophetic families! We need them in our day. I believe that a whole generation of prophets is being raised up for this very hour in history. We are becoming part of the great end-time drama foretold in the Scriptures. We are coming to a place where our sons and daughters will prophecy, have visions, dream dreams and speak the word of the Lord into a dark and hurting world. As such, the time has come for prophets and prophecy to be respected and treated well by the Church, in the Church and for the Church, for the sake of Jesus and His future bride – us.

Chapter Seven

Rebuilding a Prophetic Community

G od, the Father, has made prophecy a very important part of His purposes – He loves to speak to His children. As such, developing a safe place for prophets to grow is of vital interest to Him. The Father wants prophets to be able to grow into full maturity without suffering abuse, neglect or rejection. Prophets will endure much suffering from a world that doesn't want to hear from God, they shouldn't have to suffer this in their family or among the church community.

God designed the Church to be reflection of His family on earth. The Church is to be in the image of Jesus Christ. Christ is the pattern that the Father has give to every person on planet earth to follow. When we see Jesus, we are seeing the perfect Son walking in perfect obedience to His Father. This is why the Father has highly exalted Christ and given Him a name which is above every name. The Son chose to obey the Father fully and completely, and through this same obedience, the Son was able to establish a place on earth, the Church, comprised of the God's children.

As John the Apostle said, "Behold what manner of love the Father hath bestowed upon us, that we should be called the sons of God: therefore the world knoweth us not because it knew Him not." We are the sons of God, born and bred from heaven, to build the kingdom of God on earth. This should be the passion of the every member of the church: to build the kingdom of God, furthering the family of God for generations, until Jesus Christ returns.

The Church is the family of God, a totally new nation of chosen men and women who have been called out of darkness into the light of God's Son. God, in His sovereignty, has chosen to speak about the church through the nation of Israel. In fact, the Church is called the Israel of God by

Paul in the book of Galatians (By the way, I do not believe in replacement theology that teaches that the Church replaces Israel. However, I do believe there are many things we can learn from Israel about the way God designed the Church to function.) As such, I would like to take a look at the nation of Israel in Scripture.

Possessing Your Inheritance

Israel was made of up families formed into twelve tribes under the names of Jacob's sons. All were the seed of Abraham and each tribe was called to possess different parts of the Promised Land. God chose their inheritance for them and gave each tribe its Land of Promise. Once given their inheritance, they were called to possess it. Within the Land of Promise, there were giants seeking to prevent them from possessing the Promised Land that God had given to them. These giants actually ruled in this Promised Land.

The children of Israel needed to defeat these giants in order to prosper in God's purposes. Upon defeating these giants, Israel began to establish communities in the Promised Land where their families could grow, prosper and be blessed. Among Israel's communities were prophetic communities where the Schools of the

Prophets resided. These prophetic communities were called by God to further the prophetic ministry in Israel.

Why is it important to understand that there are prophetic communities in Israel called to promote and preserve the prophetic ministry for Israel? As we understand God's calling upon the Israelites to promote and preserve the prophetic ministry, we can then understand the calling of God upon the Church to promote and preserve the prophetic ministry. And, if God has chosen to promote and preserve prophets in the context of prophetic communities through Israel's history, it makes sense that He will do a similar thing today.

What am I saying then? I am saying that God has chosen to raise prophets up through prophetic families in the midst of prophetic communities. This was foundational for the prophetic ministry in Israel and it is foundational for the prophetic ministry in the Church today. The Church and its leaders need to realize that having a strong, fully functioning prophetic community in our midst is to our advantage. We need prophets and God knows this. This is why He has chosen to raise up prophetic communities in the earth: to preserve and propagate the prophetic ministry.

Prophets: Mission Critical Personnel

Prophets are vital to the growth of the Church. We need prophets, for without them nothing, and I do mean nothing, will happen. Prophets are catalysts for change. When prophets speak, their words bring about radical change in the earth. And, this is what we need in our day: Prophets to speak a genuine word from God that will bring about radical change in the earth and "root out, and to pull down, and to destroy, and to throw down, to build and to plant."

The prophetic word is a powerful source for change in the earth. Prophets bring the word of the Lord which enables us to do the work of God. The light and revelation contained in the words prophets speak bring us into position where we can understand the ways of God and walk in a world darkened by sin. Prophets through their words bring a taste of heaven into the realm of earth. The earth itself can become subject to the word of a prophet, for the word of God created all things.

Prophets are vital to God's mission for the Church. We need prophets, and in order for them to do all that they are called to do by God in the earth, there are tools that they need to function in their ministry. What are the tools that prophets need to fulfill their mission on earth? Prophets need the support structure of strong families and communities that strengthen them in the gift that God has given to them. In other words, prophets need strong connections through divinely established relationships. Without this, prophets can be lead astray and fall into the trap that Elijah suffered where he thought he alone was left. Elijah thought he was the only one serving and worshipping God. We need to hear God's answer to Elijah, for it is still the same answer as He is speaking today.

You're Not the Lone Ranger

Prophets have never been called to be loners. This is a common misconception in the Church today, and contradicts what the Scriptures teach. Prophets were always raised in prophetic families in the greater context of a prophetic community. This was the foundation for the prophetic office in Israel, and it is the foundation for the prophetic office in the Church today. By understanding this, we can avoid many of the pitfalls presently plaguing the prophetic office in the Church today.

Why have I said all this? Because, I believe that it is important for us to understand the relationship prophets are to have in the greater context of the Church. The Church is a community of believers called out by God to establish His kingdom on earth. Within the context of this called out community of believers, the Church, there should be a smaller community of prophets and prophetic people whom God has called to relate to one another. This is the prophetic community that I am talking about in this chapter.

God has called prophets to relate to one another. This is why the Scriptures tells us to "let the prophets speak two or three and let the other judge." In other words, God has designed prophets to be held accountable by other prophets. This is why the Bible says, "The spirits of the prophets are subject to the prophets." The Word of God is very plain on this matter; prophets are to hold one another accountable in their ministration of words of prophecy.

In order for there to be this kind of accountability, there needs to be a depth of relationship that does not currently exist amongst prophets today. And I do not believe, as some have proposed, that this will change with the advent of the apostolic office. In fact, I believe for there to be a genuine release of apostles in the

Church today, there must first be a restoration of prophets to their rightful leadership role in the Church. Without this, apostles will spin their wheels in attempting to change the Church. In the end, they will eventually succumb to the spirit of control out of frustration.

True Apostolic and Prophetic Authority

Apostles cannot enter their true place of authority in the Church until prophets have been restored to their rightful place of authority in the Church. Many have tried to claim that we are in the midst of an apostolic reformation. And, although I believe that God is in the process of restoring apostles to the Church, I do not believe there cannot be a full restoration of apostles till there has first been a full restoration of prophets. When prophets are restored to their place of authority within the Church, then apostles will also be restored to their place of authority in the Church.

God longs for the day when prophets and apostles are restored to the Church. When this happens, much of division that we presently see in the Church will end. Strife that has separated the Church for over 2000 years will cease and there will be a new level of peace in God's house.

At this time, the Lord will raise up His Church, His house, to be a house of prayer for all nations. This is the calling of Christ upon the Church: A place where all peoples of the earth will flow to the throne of God.

The Bible says, "And it shall come to pass in the last days, that the mountain of the Lord's house shall be established in the top of the moutains, and shall be exalted above the hills; and all nations shall flow to it. And many people shall go and say, 'Come ye, and let us go up to the house of the God of Jacob; and He will teach us of His ways, and we will walk in His paths: for out of Zion shall go forth the law, and the word of the Lord from Jerusalem.'"

What an awesome prophet picture painted by Isaiah of what God is about to do in our days. According to God's word, we will experience a revival unlike the world has known. All previous revivals like Azusa Street, The Welch Revival and The Great Awakening will be eclipsed by a revival unlike the world has ever known. This revival will become so widespread that it will impact all the nations of the world. People will do nothing but dwell on the things of the kingdom of God. The earth will be consumed with the fire of His glory. We are on the verge of something more awesome that this world has ever known – a revelation of the kingdom of God.

Love is the Master Key

When the Saints become a community of believers who love one another as Christ loves His Church, the world will literally beat a pathway to our doors. Unprecedented conversions will take place. The lost will be found, the sick will be healed, the blind will see and the lame shall leap for joy. The Church will be filled with the glorious sound of the voice of the Lord, and all men shall see Him whom they have slain by their sin.

Prior to this occurrence, there will be a prophetic community rebuilt within the Church. This prophetic community will have eyes to see and ears to hear the sound of the voice of the Lord. We will witness such things in these prophetic communities that fear will fall upon the Church, for God will show us that He is in His house. As in the days of Obed-edom, when the ark of the covenant abode in his house, so also will the blessing of God be so overwhelming upon prophets and prophetic communities that the entire Church will come to the doors of prophets looking for God's blessing.

Leaders of the Church at that time will be so overwhelmed by the needs of the people, and the blessing of God among prophets and prophetic community so evident, that they will long to build relationships with prophets and prophetic communities. When this happens, pastors and leaders will begin seeking God as to how they can bring prophets back into the Church. As pastors and leaders bring the prophets back into the Church in the right way, it will open the door and pave the way for apostles and apostolic ministry. Then, the Church will become an awesome army with banners as described in the book of Song of Solomon.

Jesus longs for this day, and He is looking forward to the part His prophets will play in preparing His bride. The prophetic office will be a forerunner preparing the way for Messiah Yeshua to return. This means that it is essential for the prophetic office to be restored to the Church. God is working to restore prophets to their fullness of position, power and prestige in the kingdom of God. Although the world may jeer and sneer at God's prophets, this should not be the case in God's kingdom or Church. God's prophets should be respected, honored and revered in the kingdom of God, for the part they play in helping facilitate Christ's return to receive His bride.

Prophetic Strongholds for God

Prophets are important to the plan of God. As such, they must become important to the plans of the Church. The Church needs what prophets bring. We cannot reach full maturity without the prophetic office and ministry. God desires for His people to become a prophetic people who are able to hear and see what He is saying and doing, speaking as the oracles of God. This is our holy calling in Christ: To apprehend the person of Christ till Christ becomes our all in all. Prophets help us do this.

As such, seeing the prophetic office raised up in the greater context of a prophetic community within the Church is extremely important to purposes of God. Rebuilding the prophetic community is on the heart of God. God wants His people to be prophetic. For this to happen prophets must be raised up in the greater context of a prophetic community that loves and esteems what prophets bring to the Church. Hence, we need to learn how to cooperate with God in this process of rebuilding a genuine prophetic community.

Many modern day prophets have already started doing this, catching a glimpse into the heart of God for His people and His prophets. Some of these places have names like Shiloh Estates and Moravian Falls with leaders like Mike Bickle and Rick Joyner. These men and leaders like them are seeking to rebuild the prophetic community in our day. Their desire is to raise up a prophetic people in the greater context of a prophetic community to speak prophetically to the Church and world in our day.

This is quite a vision and not one that can be accomplished on one's own. No prophet in his right mind would seek to do this apart from the direction of God. The battles are intense, for some do not believe this to be the will of God. Men and women who oppose prophetic communities think that by fighting against them, they can prevent error from entering into the Church. Error is in the Church already, and prophetic communities are part of the solution not the problem. We need men of God who are willing to rebuild these prophetic communities.

Rebuilding a prophetic community can be a difficult and dangerous proposition. On one side lay the chasm of fanaticism and exclusivity, on the other imbalance and loss of purpose. Finding the straight and narrow way is harder than most would like to admit. Jesus said, "Enter ye in at the straight gate: for wide is the gate, and broad is the way, that leadeth to destruction, and many there be which go in thereat: Because, straight is the gate, and narrow is the way, which leadeth unto life, and few there be that find it."

What a sobering admonition to prophetic leaders today. We need to take heed in what we doing so that we don't lose our way and walk down the broad way which leads to destruction. And, there are many individuals that would like to see prophetic communities end up in the ditch, on one side or the other. Some are in the Church; others are outside of the Church. As such, we desperately need God's wisdom in how to rebuild prophetic communities, His way.

Nehemiah: A Pattern for Building

I believe that God has given us a pattern book whereby we can see prophetic communities rebuilt. The book of Nehemiah will, I believe, provide us with the necessary wisdom and insight needed to see prophetic communities rebuilt and restored in today's Church.

Before we further, I would like to ask God to give us ears to hear what His Spirit is saying. We are going to need God's help and wisdom as we address this task of rebuilding prophetic communities within the Church today. My hope is that what I am writing will help those who are called to rebuild prophetic communities in the Church today. My desire is to provide this generation of leaders and future generations of leaders with the wisdom and scriptural basis for what they are doing.

Why are we looking at the book of Nehemiah? Because, Nehemiah did something that any one of us would view as impossible today: He rebuilt the walls of Jerusalem, a seemingly impossible task, in the midst of Israel's enemies, in about 30 days. Talk about wisdom, he provided the leadership of Israel the necessary wisdom to help rebuild the walls of protection around their beloved city, Jerusalem. Nehemiah did the impossible against impossible odds, and, in the end, fulfilled his mission, a mission to which God had called him. And, he did this in an amazingly short period of time.

I praise God for men like Nehemiah who have gone before us and done God's work the right way. Through their leadership, we can gain valuable insights on how we should fulfill our impossible mission. God wants us to fulfill the mission for which He has called us. He doesn't want us to start rebuilding a prophetic community only to falter and fail in the end. For this reason, God has provided us with the best of the best in leadership instruction through the life of Nehemiah. We would do well to learn what the seeds of his life convey regarding accomplishing our impossible mission.

What does Nehemiah's life teach us about accomplishing our mission to rebuild prophetic communities? I believe Nehemiah's life teaches us several things, including the fact that we cannot rebuild prophetic communities without God's help or call. God must be the one who calls and commissions us to do this specialized work for Him. Establishing prophetic communities cannot be done by the faint of heart. We will need the inward strength and witness that comes from knowing that God has called us to do the task at hand.

Supernatural Resources

Yet, it takes more than strength and inward conviction to establish a prophetic community; it takes wisdom from above, the wisdom contained in the book of Nehemiah. What kinds of things can prophetic leaders about rebuilding prophetic communities from Nehemiah? I believe there are several main things that we can learn from the book of Nehemiah, which are, His calling, His prayer life, His repentance for sin, His removal of sin from leadership and the people, and His wisdom and work ethic in rebuilding the walls with the help of the people.

Nehemiah knew he was called to do this work because God placed such an overwhelming conviction into his heart. He was filled with this inward knowledge that he was personally called to leave the man he was serving and begin leading Israel in their rebuilding efforts. One thing I would like you to see is that he was serving prior to being called to serve God in this capacity. God looks for leaders who are servants to do this kind of work. Nehemiah was a servant and as such God called him to do this impossible task. And, part of the confirmation that he was called by God was the fact that his current leader was willing to release him to do this work and also provide the resources necessary to do this work.

The work of God always require supernatural resources to be accomplished. A man or woman of God who is called by God to do a specific work will not lack in that work to which they are called. They may have to fast and prayer to receive what

God wants them to have but God will always come through and provide what they need to accomplish Him work. Nehemiah knew that God was behind him because the Lord established the provision for this work prior to starting the work. God wants to provide for His work in our day like He did during the days of Nehemiah through supernatural means. We need a supernatural God to do a work like the one being talked about in this book.

Nehemiah was able to receive God's provision through his prayer life. Nehemiah was a man of intense prayer. Prayer always brings with it the necessary provision to accomplish the work of God. A man of prayer has unlimited resources through God to accomplish His work. And, if we desire to rebuild prophetic communities for Christ we will need to pray them into existence through prayers of faith and repentance. Prayer is the link between us and God in this work to which He has called us.

Nehemiah prayed for God to bring the right leaders to his side, and God did. Nehemiah prayed for God to forgive Israel for their sin, and He did. Nehemiah prayed against His enemies, and they were defeated. Throughout the entire book of Nehemiah, we see the results of his prayers. Nehemiah's prayer prepared the way for the repentance that was needed by the people for their sin.

Sin always prevents the rebuilding of God's work. Until sin is dealt with in the camp we are open to our enemies. Nehemiah knew how to lead the people into repentance, by first repenting himself for his own sin and the sins of his fathers. Nehemiah knew that unless he confessed his own sins, others would not be willing to confess their sins. He did this openly in the sight of God and the people. Nehemiah was ruthless toward his own sin. He did not call it something that it was not. He called it what it was sin. We will first need to deal with our sins before we can help others deal with their sins so that we can see prophetic communities rebuilt in the Church today.

There is much sin among prophets today. Prophets have not taken responsibility for their actions as they should. We have made many mistakes and people have paid the price for our errors. We have believed and promoted lies, tolerating sin in the camp for far too long. God forgive us for the wrongs that we have done. We need to come to a place of repentance as prophets for what we have done and what others have done in the name of the prophetic. For this to happen, we need prophetic leaders, like Nehemiah, who are willing to acknowledge their sin, confess it openly and receive forgiveness and cleansing from the hand of God. Remember, we do what we do in the sight of God, not men, for the purpose of bringing men into right relationship with God. We need leaders with the boldness necessary to do this.

Freedom From Sin

Truthfully, there is more sin in the Church today than there has ever been in previous generations. And, our own prayerlessness is a witness against us of the sin in our hearts. God forbid that we should be judged as a Church today. Although there is much talk about prayer there is little actual effectual fervent prayer taking place among leaders and believers. Would to God that this would change. It must change if there are to be prophetic communities rebuilt in the Church today. We need praying prophets to lead prophetic families into rebuilding prophetic communities. God's charge to us is, "Handle with Prayer."

In this construction process, there will be problems that occur. Things will happen that will seek to divert our attention from the call of God.

We cannot let this happen. We must be ruthless in dealing with the sin that divides us amongst leaders in prophetic communities. A little leaven can cause entire community problems if left unchecked. Sin is the only thing that can prevent God's blessing from enabling us to build. When a leader sins, he must be rebuked. If this sin is in public, he may need to be rebuked publicly. Nehemiah did this: he rebuked leaders within Israel for holding their brothers and sisters as slaves to debts which should have been forgiven by them.

The year of Jubilee had come and gone. People should have been rejoicing over their freedom. Instead, leaders were holding people in bondage to debts that they had already been freed from by law. Can you see how debilitating this was to the work of God? In the same way, unforgiveness among leaders can cause the entire work of God to suffer needlessly. We should have forgiveness in our hearts and be setting people free not holding them in bondage for the things they have done. We cannot serve Christ if we use ungodly means to hold people captive to our rule. Prophets cannot use the sins they see to hold people in bondage to their past, they must learn to speak redemptively. This is the wisdom we need among the prophets within the prophetic communities that we are rebuilding.

The Spirit Brings Liberty

God's wisdom says, "Set my people free." The devil's wisdom says, "Hold people back and keep them in bondage." We cannot rebuild people's lives if we hold them in bondage to their past. We must choose to let them go and set them free. Our choice is the one that places us on the right road to see prophetic communities rebuilt. If we are willing to forgive those who have sinned against us, we can help restore them into their position in Christ as prophets in the midst of a prophetic people who are rebuilding a prophetic community. Then, they will be willing to work in the rebuilding process.

Free people are people who are willing to work. A people in bondage dreads the work they do, for they know that they are being used and abused by those who are leading them. We cannot be abusive in our leadership style, otherwise those under our care will not be willing to do the work necessary in the rebuilding process. Instead they will bring with them the seeds of insurrection and rebellion under the load they are carrying. We do not want this to happen. We need to use wisdom so that people are willing to do what God has called them to do.

Work will be required if prophetic communities are to be restored. This process of restoration will not happen by accident, it will happen by choice. I believe that this rebuilding process is worth the price necessary to see it accomplished. However, not everyone in our midst will feel this way. Some will only be in it for the blessing they receive. Choose your connections wisely. Very often, the good is the enemy of the best. A good choice may lead us down the wrong path in this rebuilding process. Nehemiah was constantly confronted by Tobiah whose name means, "God is good." The good can be the enemy of the best. Don't allow the good to hold you back from God's best. Choose wisely!

Nehemiah chose wisely, and as a result was able to accomplish God's purpose for his life which was to rebuild the walls of Jerusalem. We too can accomplish God's purpose for our lives if we choose to give heed to God's wisdom. This is why we should surround ourselves with those who will hold us accountable for the decisions we make. We should not surround ourselves with 'yes' men and women. We need people around us who will think wisely, act righteously and do justly with humility and love. This is what prophets called to raise up and rebuild prophetic schools and communities should look for as they choose those around them.

In Closing

My prayer for leaders called to this work is that God would surround, protect and bless you in your divine calling. I pray that you would not settle for less than the best, and that you would always surround yourselves with the cream of the crop not the bottom of the barrel. I pray that God would guide you daily in the choices you make so that at the end of your life you may hear the words, "Well done, My good and faithful servant, enter into the joy of your Lord."

In closing, I hope this book has been a blessing to you. I trust that you have learned from what I have written and gleaned through the things that I have shared. I hope to meet all of you some day in the courts of heaven and trust that this book will be recorded as one of those that helped God's end-time people accomplish His will. Amen.

Appendix

Guide to Helpful Prophetic Resources

1. *How to Know if Your Prophecy is Really from God and What to Do if It Is* (Scott Wallis, Xulon Press, ISBN: 1931232415, Available at Lighthouse-Publications.com)

2. *Plugging into the Spirit of Prophecy: Adding Power to Your Prophetic Words* (Scott Wallis, Xulon Press, ISBN: 1931232210, Available at Lighthouse-Publications.com)

3. *Prophets and Personal Prophecy (Book 1)* (Bill Hamon, Destiny Image Publishers, ISBN: 0939868032)

4. *Prophets and Personal Prophecy (Book 3)* (Bill Hamon, Destiny Image Publishers, ISBN: 0939868059)

5. *The Sound of His Voice* (Kim Clement, Charisma House, ISBN: 088419339X)

6. *The Voice of God* (Cindy Jacobs, Regal Books, ISBN: 0830717730)

7. *Surprised by the Voice of God* (Jack Deere, Zondervan, ISBN: 0310225582)

8. *You Can Hear the Voice of God* (Steve Sampson, Chosen Books, ISBN: 0800793331)

9. *The Ministry Anointing of the Prophet* (John Eckhardt, Crusaders Publications, ISBN: 0963056727)

10. *Developing Your Prophetic Gifting* (Graham Cooke, Chosen Books, ISBN: 0800793269)

11. *Prophetic Gatherings in the Church* (David Blomgren, Bible Temple Publishing, ISBN: 0914936360)

12. *You May All Prophesy* (Steve Thompson, Destiny Image Publishers, ISBN: 1878327968)

13. *Prayer Shield* (Peter Wagner, Regal Books, ISBN: 0830715142)

14. *User Friendly Prophecy* (Larry Randolph, Destiny Image Publishers, ISBN: 1560436956)

15. *Your Sons and Daughters Shall Prophesy* (Ernest Gentile, Chosen Books, ISBN: 0800792696)

16. *Dialogue with God* (Mark Virkler, Destiny Image Publishers, ISBN: 0882706209)

Other Books Available from Lighthouse Publications

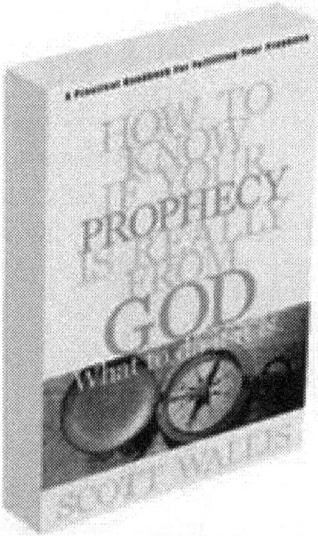

How to Know if Your Prophecy is Really from God

One of the most important books on prophecy available for Believers. If you have ever received a prophetic word, then this book will help you discern if that word was from God, and if it was, what to do with it to see if fulfilled.

Author: Scott Wallis
Retail Price: $11.99
ISBN: 1931232415

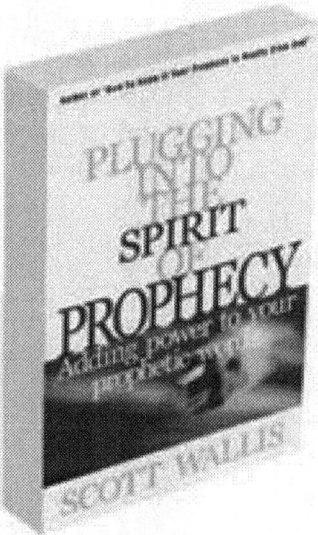

Plugging into the Spirit of Prophecy

God has designed every believer to walk in the prophetic. You can learn how to flow in the Holy Spirit of prophecy. This exciting book will teach you how to do this and more. You will experience God's awesome power through the prophetic word.

Author: Scott Wallis
Retail Price: $11.99
ISBN: 1931232210

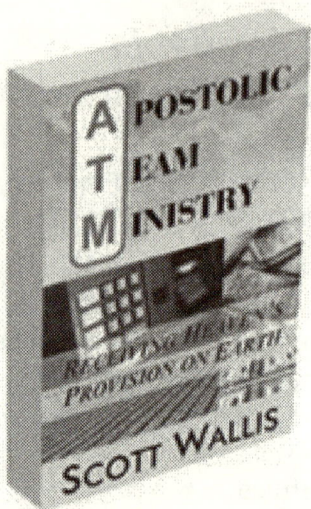

Apostolic Team Ministry

Pastor/Prophet Scott Wallis provides practical answers to the questions that many believers have, such as: "How can I overcome lack in my life?" Learn why apostles are so important to the purpose and plans of God, and how apostolic teams release tremendous supernatural power and wealth into the Church.

Author: Scott Wallis
Retail Price: $11.99
ISBN: 0964221128

The Third Reformation is Coming

Prophetic leaders have been declaring for several years that a third reformational movement of the Holy Spirit was about to begin. Find out what this third reformation is and how it will radically change the Church and your life.

Author: Scott Wallis
Retail Price: $9.99
ISBN: 0964221144

170

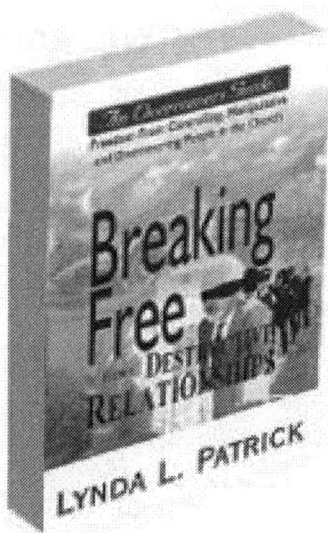

Breaking Free from Destructive Relationships

Lynda Patrick explains the facets of spiritual control and abuse that so many believers face, giving insights into the beginnings and outcomes. She exposes the Jezebel spirit, and articulates the remedies that will "set free the mind and spirit...to the eternal purposes that were predetermined...before the abuse even took place."

Authors: Lynda L. Patrick
Retail Price: $14.99
ISBN: 193365600X

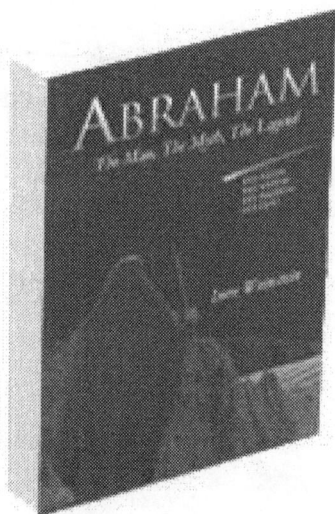

Abraham: The Man, The Myth, The Legend

A fictional account of Abraham's early years, based in a Biblical worldview. All the wonder of God's redemption in the life of a young pagan man, his glorious romance with Sarai, the exciting action of battles and rescue encounters, and his discovery of the one true God of the universe.

Authors: Imre Weinstein
Retail Price: $19.99
Pre-Order Price: $13.99
ISBN: 1933656018

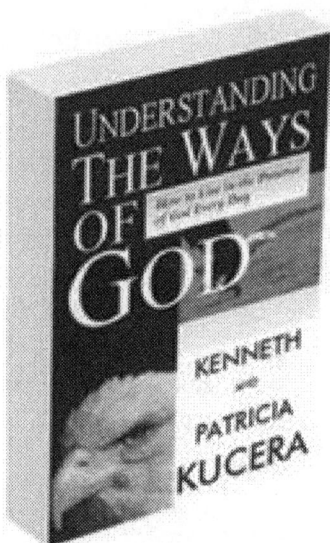

Understanding the Ways of God

You can understand the mysteries behind God's ways. No longer wonder why God does what He does – you can know. As you read this exciting book, you will learn secret after secret of walking in the ways of God. Unlock the potential God has placed inside of you as you learn the ways of God!

Authors: Ken & Pat Kucera
Retail Price: $11.99
ISBN: 0964221152

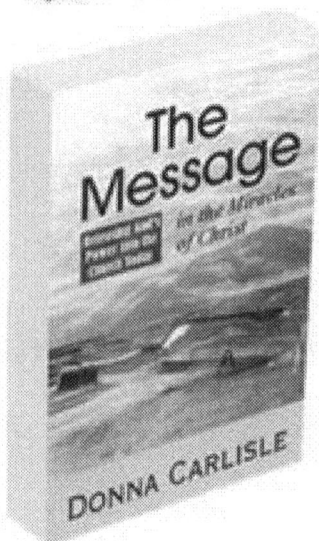

The Message in the Miracles of Christ

Recently, researchers have discovered that there may be hidden coded messages in the actual text of the Bible. Could it be that the miracles of Jesus also reveal hidden messages of what God is doing in our day? Discover the answer as you read this exciting book!

Author: Donna Carlisle
Retail Price: $14.99
ISBN: 0964221136

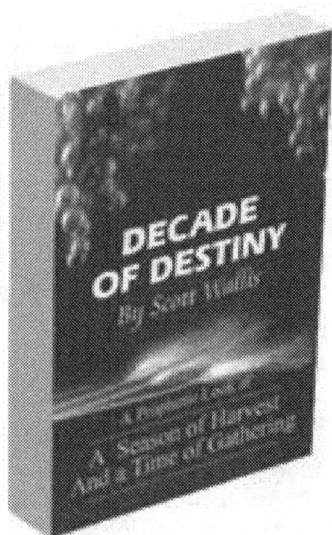

Decade of Destiny

A powerful prophetic word detailing what God is doing in our days. First written in 1991, this timeless book has proven to be an accurate window into the future. Discover what God is saying to His Church today!

Author: Scott Wallis
Retail Price: $11.99
ISBN: 0964221195

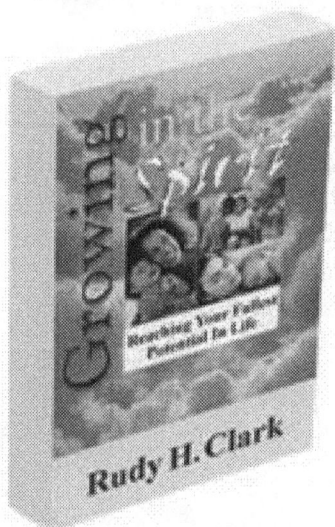

Growing in the Spirit

Taking from life examples, Pastor/Prophet Rudy Clark reveals principles of spiritual growth. Through many life lessons, God has taught Reverend Clark the values and virtues that have made him the man he is today. Experience freedom as you learn how to reach your fullest potential.

Author: Rudy H. Clark
Retail Price: $14.99
ISBN: 0964221160

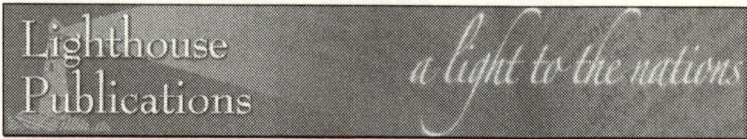

• Additional Resources •

www.ingramcontent.com/pod-product-compliance
Lightning Source LLC
LaVergne TN
LVHW011326080426
835513LV00006B/211